Frontispiece: Fyodor Chaliapin as Dosifey at the Maryinsky, St Petersburg, in 1911, in a production by Diaghilev conducted by Albert Coates. Diaghilev's production toured to Paris and London, where Chaliapin sang the role at the Theatre Royal, Drury Lane in 1913.

This Opera Guide is sponsored by

48

Khovanshchina
The Khovansky Affair

Modest Musorgsky

Editors: Jennifer Batchelor and Nicholas John
Opera Guide Series Editor: Nicholas John

Calder Publications Limited
Riverrun Press Inc.
Paris · London · New York

Published in association with English National Opera

COPYRIGHT DATA

First published in Great Britain, 1994, by Calder Publications Limited 179 King's Cross Road, London WC1X 9BZ

Published in the U.S.A., 1994, by Riverrun Press Inc., 1170 Broadway, New York, NY 10001

Copyright © English National Opera, 1994

Apocalypse Then, Now and (For Us) Never: Reflections on Musorgsky's Other Historical Opera © Caryl Emerson 1994

Musorgsky's Music of Time © Gerard McBurney 1994

'Khovanshchina' in context © Rosamund Bartlett 1994

'The Khovansky Affair' English translation © Carol Borah Palca 1994

ALL RIGHTS RESERVED

ISBN 0 7145 4278 4

BRITISH LIBRARY CATALOGUING IN PUBLICATION DATA is available

LIBRARY OF CONGRESS CATALOGUING IN PUBLICATION DATA is available

English National Opera receives financial assistance from the Arts Council of England.

Typeset in Britain by Books Unlimited (Nottm), Rainworth, Notts, NG21 0JE

Printed by Ebenezer Baylis Ltd, Worcester.

CONTENTS

LIST OF ILLUSTRATIONS

Frontispiece: Chaliapin as Dosifey at the Maryinsky, St Petersburg, in 1911.

Apocalypse Then, Now, and (For Us) Never: Reflections on Musorgsky's Other Historical Opera

Caryl Emerson

In April 1881, one month after Musorgsky's death, Rimsky-Korsakov was doing an inventory on his deceased friend's manuscripts and unfinished projects. 'Once it's cleaned up a bit, *Khovanshchina* could be orchestrated,' he wrote to his friend Semyon Kruglikov, Moscow professor and well-known music critic. 'But good lord, what a subject!'

A century later, that paradox still stands. From the gorgeously mellifluous prelude, 'Dawn over the Moscow River', through a series of sinuous and tenacious melodies for both solo and chorus, the opera has the makings of a lyrical masterpiece; it is the best testimony we have that after *Boris Godunov* Musorgsky was moving ever further away from the declamatory realism of the 'Mighty Handful' toward a new operatic aesthetic.[1] But as Rimsky intimated, the subject matter – the plot – retained the abrupt transitions, discontinuities, nitty-gritty violence and prosaic chattiness characteristic of Musorgsky's earlier naturalistic musical narratives. Consider only the First Act. The Dawn overture gives way to drunken musketeers recounting whom they had drawn, quartered or crushed with stones the night before: lyricism prevails only as long as the protagonists sleep or dream. Once they wake up, it is non-stop denunciations, violence, cynicism, self-interest and political intrigue. These themes are frequently clothed in lyrical form and surrounded by rich melodies, often to hypocritical effect. What love there is belongs to the visionary, not to the incarnated, world.

There are, however, problems with *Khovanshchina* more serious than the brutality of its Muscovite politics – which have enabled a series of brilliant meddlings even more invasive than the scandalous reworkings of *Boris*. Musorgsky left this second historical opera largely unorchestrated and incomplete at crucial junctures (the end of Act Two and the finale), thus clearing the way for talented interpreters, from Nikolai Rimsky-Korsakov to Serge Diaghilev and Dmitry Shostakovich, to rework the musical materials into a coherent dramatic concept. One famous example will suffice. For the Paris première in 1913, Diaghilev restructured the entire work as a 'choral opera': the chatty Act Two was omitted altogether, Igor Stravinsky and Maurice Ravel were asked to prepare a new score that inconsistently fitted Musorgskian gestures back into the Rimskian fabric, and Stravinsky was commissioned to arrange, out of Musorgsky's unfinished sketches for the final act, an Old Believer

---

1. See Taruskin, *Musorgsky: Eight Essays and an Epilogue* (1993). In his Introduction, Taruskin weans his hero from the image of 'radical democrat in decline' that has coloured our interpretation of Musorgsky's final half-decade; and in Chapter 7 he makes a strong case for *Khovanshchina* as an aristocratic, deeply pessimistic national tragedy rather than the pasted-up and contradictory 'folk drama' it is often taken to be. Taruskin's arguments supplement and improve upon my own reading in 'Musorgsky's Libretti on Historical Themes: From the Two *Boris*es to *Khovanshchina*', in *Reading Opera*, ed. Groos and Parker (1988).

chorus with which to close the opera.[2] This chorus would replace the famous brassy trumpet fanfare that Rimsky had invented to end the opera on an upbeat, Westernizing, 'Petrine' note. But Chaliapin protested against any tampering with Rimsky's versions and the Stravinsky chorus fell by the wayside; it was revived and attached to the Shostakovich orchestration by Claudio Abbado in his 1989 Vienna Staatsoper production, thereby re-entering the repertory as an option for future revivals of the opera.

No less problematic for audience and composer was the historical material itself. Unlike in his earlier *Boris Godunov* – co-authored, as it were, with the dramatic genius of Alexander Pushkin – in *Khovanshchina*, Musorgsky worked with no literary source text at all, cobbling a libretto together out of songs, scraps of published histories and raw historical documents. The events at issue here (1682-1698) are, if anything, even more complex and ideologically diffuse than the Time of Troubles that had engulfed Boris Godunov and Dmitry the Pretender ninety years earlier. With characteristic eccentricity, Musorgsky declined to use this chaotic history as mere backdrop, as something to set off more operatically-focused personal stories; he granted all the squabbling social groups of seventeenth-century Muscovy equal weight in the opera and sank the plot deep into documented events.

To be sure, these events are conflated and at times enriched with fictional persons. But oddly, such poetic licence does not make things easier to follow, nor does it facilitate the sense of a forward-moving plot. On the contrary, stasis and a sense of predetermination are the ruling mood; parties confront each other continually, enunciating their own truths, in almost total non-communication. Most radically (if we are to credit the surviving authorial sketches for the final scene), Musorgsky refused to follow the conventional organizing principle for the end of a historical opera, whether Beethoven's *Fidelio*, Berlioz's *Les Troyens* or Borodin's *Prince Igor*: he did not permit any resolution on the erotic plane, any mere consummation of love between hero and heroine, to resolve problems on the historical plane. As we shall see, the philosophy of love enunciated in *Khovanshchina* is one of its most remarkable achievements, fully as powerful and compassionate as Musorgsky's philosophy of history is non-progressive and enfeebling.

My reading of the opera is structured around this competition – an ancient one in opera, but here given a horrifying turn – between the 'love plot' and the 'history plot'. For the former, we have only two representatives: the Old Believers Marfa and Dosifey and their understanding of love as fidelity, obedience to fate, perseverance in this life and transcendence beyond it into the next. The history plot, on the contrary, is one uninterrupted seam of denunciations, hypocrisies, and false pretensions to the control of events. Perhaps paradoxically, all its major figures share

2. I am indebted here to R. W. Oldani, who has worked with Diaghilev's manuscript archive in an attempt to reconstruct the Paris première. For details of this 1913 production and scandals surrounding Diaghilev, Stravinsky, Andrei Rimsky-Korsakov and Chaliapin, see J. Vershinina, 'Musorgskii i Stravinskii (O diagilevskoi postanovke "Khovanshchiny")', in *M.P. Musorgskii i muzyka XX veka* (Moscow: Myzyka, 1990); in English, see Richard Taruskin's "Note on the Final Chorus", in 'The Power of the Black Earth' essay for the Deutsche-Grammophon CD (1989).

a narrowly blind focus on the world; actors in history, they see only the immediate events and mortal insults of the present.

A few words, then, about the real past that animates the operatic episodes. The time is the seventeenth century, the decade just preceding Russia's first full-scale attempt to westernize by government decree (the reign of Peter the Great, 1689-1725). The 1680s were the most unsettled and threatening years the Russian state had known since 1610-13 – when the founding of the House of Romanov formally put an end to the *Smuta* or 'Time of Troubles', the violent interregnum that had swallowed up Boris Godunov. State-sponsored reform in the Russian Orthodox Church had triggered mass resistance among the conservative faithful, who refused to countenance any change in details of holy writ or ritual. After 1666 – the Apocalyptic Year of the Beast – groups of schismatics or 'True Believers' (dubbed 'Old Believers' by their enemies) had been preparing for the End of the World, which for them mandated absolute non-cooperation with the fallen and demonic state. The self-immolation of religious communities in oiled retreats became ever more common. Antichrist was expected at any time; he was soon to be embodied in the clean-shaven, cunningly secular Peter the First.

The major part of the opera's action, and most of the historical documents embedded in the libretto, date from 1682, a year of succession crisis and almost constant turmoil. The young tsar Fyodor Alekseyevich had just died, and families of the two competing dowager-tsaritsas each put forward their surviving sons. One was the sickly adolescent Ivan, whose elder sister Sophia, of the powerful Miloslavsky clan, was ambitious, ugly, and politically astute; the other was the robust nine-year-old Peter of the Naryshkin family, under the uncertain protection of a much less gifted mother and uncles. Although Peter was at first favoured in the struggle, the militia in Moscow (known as *Streltsy* or musketeers, a restless and undisciplined crew) rallied behind Ivan and secured joint sovereignty for the half-brothers with Sophia as regent. *Khovanshchina* opens at this historical moment. (The initial denunciation concocted by Shaklovity in Act One – fabricated denunciations being something of a signature theme in the history plot – addresses dual 'imperial majesties'.) The Streltsy were led by Prince Ivan Khovansky, an old-style Muscovite patriarch with a harem on his estate and crude political ambitions in the capital. Prince Khovansky used his influence to oppose the Church reforms (thereby allying himself with the Old Belief) and also, perhaps, to make his own bid for the throne. Sensing a threat to her power, Sophia successfully arranged for her current lover, the boyar Fyodor Shaklovity, to trap the Khovanskys. Father and son were both executed for treason in 1682.

When the Streltsy rose in protest against these executions, Sophia bought back their loyalty by pardoning their indiscretions and appointing Shaklovity as their leader. (The regent was a formidable woman: she simultaneously courted the support of the old nobility while promoting as her chief minister Prince Vasily Golitsyn, of a sophisticated westernized noble family.) At this point, the opera plot becomes something of a free variation on Russian seventeenth-century political history. For, into this turbulent 1682 shell, the composer introduced events from later death to Shaklovity, exile to Golitsyn, and dispatched Sophia to a convent; and 1698, the final Streltsy revolt that brought Tsar Peter back from Europe in high rage, this time willing to build mass gallows on Red Square for the remaining musketeers. The plot is a nightmare of cross-hatched loyalties.

To add further to this complexity, the very cast of characters was problematic for Russian musical art in the nineteenth century. Since 1845, Imperial Law Codes had forbidden the representation of ecclesiastical personages in dramatic productions, and in 1837 a casual ruling by Emperor Nicholas I became grounds for prohibiting the appearance on stage of any Russian tsar in an operatic role.[3] In subsequent years, this prohibition was flexed sufficiently to permit the operatic casting of *pre*-Romanov rulers (Ivan the Terrible, Boris Godunov), but one could hardly expect the ruling dynasty to licence such indignity for its greatest progenitor, Peter himself. In short, even had Musorgsky wished to bring Peter onstage in *Khovanshchina*, he could not have done so – and this worked to make the Petrine image all the more abstract, powerful, and threatening. Laws of the Empire mandated a similar blunting of the Old Believers (in the opera's few domestic productions, the schismatics were identified with religious discontent only in a most vague and indirect way). Thus, from the start, a core conflict in the opera – that between an aggressive, secularizing tsarist power and a stubbornly passive 'otherworld' of spiritual dissenters – could not be fully embodied.

Did these conditions crimp or enable Musorgsky's *Khovanshchina*? The interaction of inner creativity with outer censorship is always complex, but here the prohibitions seem to have pushed Musorgsky to visions of a very high order. To some extent his material may have forced on him the evasion and indirection we sense during major confrontations in the plot, where aggrieved representatives of all classes in Old and New Muscovy gather together and talk past (or shout at) one another until an authoritative figure from the spiritual realm – Dosifey or Marfa – arrives to dissolve the tension. But Musorgsky, one could argue, turned this principled, often incoherent, non-communication among rival social groups into a concept of history that was both coherent and tragically consistent.

Since this is an opera about apocalypse, let us begin by looking at ends. By and large, scenes in *Khovanshchina* end either in a denunciation (emblematic of the history plot) or in prayer – which connotes fidelity, renunciation, submission to fate, and love. The opera alternates between these two genres with some precision. Act One opens with the writing of a false denunciation, which is then launched on a life of its own. In quick succession, we witness wanton violence against the scribe, his coerced reading of a publicly-posted list of condemned traitors (in general, writing and reading do not fare well in this opera: truth is arrived at by other means), and an ugly father-son rivalry over the Lutheran girl Emma; the act closes on a chorus of Old Believers praying for protection from the Antichrist. Act Two, in which Marfa's bewitchingly authoritative performance as seer of Golitsyn's fate is balanced by the selfish, inconclusive

---

3. More on this censorship history is available in Emerson and Oldani, *Modest Musorgsky and 'Boris Godunov': Myths, Realities, Reconsiderations* (Cambridge, 1994).

'The Morning of the Streltsy execution' by Vasily Surikov, 1881

crisis years: 1689, the year of a second Streltsy revolt whose collapse brought political bickering of the opera's principal historical figures, ends abruptly on Shaklovity's announcement that the Khovanskys are under arrest for treason (the midpoint of the denunciation trajectory). Act Three opens on an Old Believer chant and ends on a prayer, this time sung by the chastened Streltsy whom the cowardly Ivan Khovansky has just abandoned to Peter's advancing troops. Act Four has two spectacular finales, both of them thoroughly political: in the first scene, the initial denunciation on Red Square reaches its climax in the shooting (or stabbing) of Khovansky *père* amid his Persian slave girls; and in the second scene, the ghastly spectacle of the Streltsy carrying their own execution blocks ends with an unexpected pardon, a sort of cancelled or counter-denunciation, delivered in the name of the young tsars. Act Five, if experienced with Stravinsky's final chorus in place, is entirely prayer.

How is the history plot – or better, history itself as a progressive ideal – served by this arrangement of events? In general, very poorly. As Russian students of the opera have noted (and as Vladimir Stasov, indefatigable mentor and propagandist for Musorgsky's works, complained loudly to the composer), the libretto is episodic, full of vacant interactions, and has almost nothing positive to say about the political or human material destined to become the great Russian Empire of post-Napoleonic Europe. One after another, the social classes of Old Muscovy are introduced – only to discredit themselves utterly with their behaviour and their self-serving perspective on events. All groups lose or are wiped out. We should note that Musorgsky tended to mark the dynamics of both his ending modes, 'denunciation' as well as 'prayer,' *piano*; strong, historically self-confident closure (such as the celebratory finale of *Fidelio*) is simply not an option in this historical opera, which can be seen as a set of horrific variations on the theme of the Holy Fool who quietly and desperately concludes *Boris Godunov*. When Rimsky-Korsakov finished the Fifth Act with his fanfare of trumpets announcing the arrival of Peter's regiment, he certainly altered the author's concept of the opera profoundly – and one can sympathize with his reasons. As Musorgsky left *Khovanshchina*, no one on stage was destined to remain alive.

This dying-out of Russia was especially inapposite in the context of St Petersburg, 1872, when Musorgsky – still at work revising *Boris Godunov* – began sketching the plot of *Khovanshchina*. That year marked the bicentennial jubilee of Peter the Great's birth, an event noisily celebrated in the capital with much patriotic affirmation of progress and imperial accomplishment. In a letter written to Vladimir Stasov in May of that year, two weeks into the bicentennial, Musorgsky noted ruefully: 'Public benefactors are inclined to glorify themselves and to fix their glory in documents, but the people groan, and drink to stifle their groans, and groan all the louder: we're still here!' As grim illustration we have the gestating plot of *Khovanshchina*, where all politicking literally ends up in dead ends.

For a historical opera built on documented events that had led (who in the Russia of 1872 would deny it?) to a demonstrably great future, this was indeed a bleak reading of Russia's past. But it is a vision in full resonance with some of Musorgsky's other works of the mid-1870s, most especially his song cycle 'Songs and Dances of Death' (1875-1877). To construct that cycle, Musorgsky had pared away from his received song texts all traces of the distancing frame given them by their author, the poet Golenishchev-Kutuzov – that is, he deliberately removed all traces of a life (say, the life of the poet telling the story) that could have survived the deaths that occur in the songs. For Musorgsky, to be dramatically true to death in history, and even to the microhistory of a single life and its end, meant that there *could be no survivors*. There were no exempt narrators anywhere, and from that fact came the entire risk and terror of the theme.

Only prayer is large enough to confront and defeat the reality of 'death-in-history'. In *Khovanshchina* it is significant that the prayers – which, in addition to their closing function, circulate in choral blocks at the periphery of the stage, as background to the ugly details of personal or national history – often sing in the past tense, of a victory already achieved: 'We have destroyed the heresy, we have shamed it, we have defeated it, we despise it!' The Old Belief is literally not of this world. For the schismatics, all value is in an absolute past; while present struggles may indeed appear to take place and bring pain to their participants, in fact there is no contest, everything that matters has already occurred, and forever. Thus can Dosifey and Marfa turn up and apply a solvent to the petty competitions that make up everyone else's plot. Throughout the opera's first three acts – and again in an emblematic echo in the final act, at the foot of the pyre, when Andrey indulges his frivolous pursuit of Emma to the very last moment – the forces of Old Muscovy gather, grab at each other's goods, and are deadlocked. Then an Old Believer comes onstage to disperse the tension: Marfa to save Emma from Andrey, Dosifey to save Emma from both Khovanskys, Dosifey to separate Khovansky and Golitsyn and to offer protection to Marfa. Since all parties in the history plot see only their own selfish needs and speak only of their own immediate grievances, real-world issues are not so much resolved by this intervention as they are *dissolved*. (When an Old Believer appears on stage, sooner or later the squabble is diffused and the squabbling parties wander off.) Thus the authority of these otherworldly persons is not challenged, and yet, oddly, their authority is impotent to change the givens of this world. As Dosifey, their spiritual leader, sings repeatedly: True Believers are not in Russia, they are *seeking* her.

Thus love and its expression in prayer need only rarely and superficially *interact* with the history plot. Pre-apocalyptic time, the time before the End of Time in which the Old Belief lives, is patient; from its perspective, historical power is easy, for with time it simply goes away. In contrast, what we will now examine as the 'love plot' is much more complex, difficult and robust – and a token of its robustness is that it is tested and found to be superior by its rival genre from the historical realm, denunciation. In a crucial episode too often cut from the Third Act, the aging and embittered Old Believer Susanna overhears Marfa's passionate song on spurned love and impending sacrifice – and accuses the singer of seduction by unclean forces. For the sin of arousing her with carnal images and 'wicked charms', Susanna wants Marfa burned at the stake as a witch. That denunciation is immediately discredited by Dosifey, who, in an uncharacteristically unkind and violent gesture toward one of his own, banishes Susanna from his sight as a 'Daughter of

13

Helen Field (Emma) and Robin Leggate (Andrey) in 1982 at Covent Garden
(photo: Clive Barda)
Ludmilla Schemtschuk as Marfa in the 1989 Vienna Staatsoper
production (photo: Österreichischer Bundestheaterverband/
Alex Zeininger)

Belial' and the devil's spawn. The relationship between these three Old Believers in this episode, the precise midpoint of the opera, lays out a philosophy of love that could be said to work in opposition to history's forward movement – and against many of our familiar Western models of the religious life as well.

In the Christian West, celibacy, asceticism, and the inherent sinfulness of matter sit deep in mainstream post-Augustinian definitions of love. In the Eastern Church, by contrast, the body is not renounced or cast out as sinful; thus it is saved not by redemption but by compassion and transfiguration. Never sympathetic to the Cartesian dualism of spirit and matter, Eastern Orthodox philosophers preached the discrete but inseparable interdependence of the two realms. These teachings come together in the richly ambivalent image of Marfa. An Old Believer in the other world, she is also the vulnerable romantic lead in this one; as such she presents an absolutely unembarrassed fusion of carnal love with its simultaneous transcendence.[4] Surely it is this passionate investment of the body that Susanna, in her frenzy, cannot tolerate; for that reason Dosifey condemns her for responding with 'selfish pride' to her 'sister's aching heart'.

Consider the remarkable dialogue that takes place in that scene once the puritanical Susanna is driven from it. 'Endure a little longer, my dear child, and you will serve our ancient Holy Russia . . . We are seeking her,' Dosifey sings to Marfa. 'I am despised, forgotten, cast off,' she replies. 'Prince Andrey?' Dosifey inquires, knowing that the profligate and trivial Khovansky *fils* is a worthless object of Marfa's passion. 'Yes.' 'Is he annoying you?' 'He wanted to slit my throat.' 'And what would you have with him?' 'Like two of God's candles, together we shall soon burn . . .' And then Marfa, in torment over Andrey's infidelity, puts herself to the test. 'If my love is sinful and criminal,' she sings to Dosifey, 'then kill me, quickly, do not spare me, let my flesh die, through the death of the flesh my spirit will save itself.' Dosifey will have none of that. 'In God's will is our unfreedom,' he replies. 'Let us leave this place; endure, my dear child, love as you have always loved, and all that you have passed through will itself pass.'

There is no recrimination or denial, no passing of judgment on Marfa's misplaced fidelity, no sanction to separate the two realms of body and spirit. The only advice has been to wait and to go on loving: eternal values. Time will take care of the rest. It is surely no accident that, after this powerful scene, Shaklovity, that primal source of all denunciations, sings an oily and opportunistic aria in which he 'prays' – from him it can only be hypocrisy and parody – for Russia's deliverance from 'ruthless

4. For this reason it can be awkward to cast Marfa on stage: in her nun-like garb she is effective as the stern figure who saves Emma in the First Act, but singing the passionate folksong in Act Three presents problems. In the Abbado/Vienna videotaped production, she comes onstage in the second appearance dressed inappropriately in sky-blue, her head uncovered, scattering flowers. (This scandal pales, however, beside the inexplicable presence in that production of a cleanshaven Dosifey: adult Orthodox males could not enter heaven without their beards – this was a major point of contention for the modernizing Tsar Peter, who ended up taxing them – and a beardless Old Believer looks simply blasphemous, like a Jesuit.)
5. The placement of this earnestly virtuous aria in the mouth of Shaklovity has made many directors uncomfortable. In 1913, Diaghilev wanted to recast the aria for Dosifey (considering him a more appropriate singer of it than the 'arch-rascal' bureaucrat), but Chaliapin,

Paata Burchuladze as Dosifey in the 1989 Vienna Staatsoper production (photo: Österreichischer Bundestheaterverband/Alex Zeininger)

Gwynne Howell (Dosifey), Robert Tear (Golitsyn) and Evgeny Nesterenko (Khovansky) in the 1982 Covent Garden production (photo: Clive Barda)

mercenaries'.[5]

Thus does Old Believer love embrace the opera as an absolute value, but only in the context of Old Believer time. Such time is not of this world; although it registers the political and social events of the world, it need not judge itself by those events nor be captive to its chronology. The stakes here are worth our attention, for Musorgsky has been often judged wanting in the matter of musicalizing romantic love. This is true. Musorgsky's vocal 'romances' on love themes are banal and derivative; and we recall that Marina Mniszech, fiancée to Dmitry the Pretender, entered *Boris Godunov* somewhat as an afterthought (the initial 1868 version of the opera had no Polish Act and thus no romantic female lead at all, a major reason why the Imperial Theatres rejected it). Musorgsky's most startling talent was assumed to lie precisely in prosaic, non-idealized musical portraiture, and frequently of personalities that were pre- or post-Eros: children, the very old, social outcasts, exasperated wives, orphans, beggars, holy fools. But in *Khovanshchina*, as part of the greatly intensified lyricism that marks his final decade, Musorgsky took on love full-face. In the final section of this essay, I would like to suggest how the competing claims of history and of love make the Stravinsky choral ending preferable to Rimsky's worldly, self-confident trumpets in realizing the dramatic concept of the opera.[6]

The surviving sketches for Act Five (which Musorgsky last worked on in August 1880, seven months before his death) are devoted almost entirely to the increasing withdrawal, and then the transfiguration, of the Old Believers. When Rimsky-Korsakov set about reworking these materials into what was, to his mind, an effective finale, he created for this psalm-like and fragile texture a durable *this*-worldly frame. He highlighted the final exchange (or 'Love Requiem', as Musorgsky had put it) between the ecstatic Marfa and the terror-stricken Andrey; to pad out Dosifey's farewell aria at the beginning he created an additional thirty bars of text and music, in which the elder puts his people's struggle into historical perspective against a sinuous 'curling flame' theme in the orchestra. And of course he added the thrilling bugles of Peter's advance guard at the end. Let us consider in more detail the difference between the unfinished authorial sketch for the final scene and the more fully realized, 'Rimskified' version of the immolation.

In Musorgsky's notes, Dosifey opens the Act on a distanced and stylized lament. In Rimsky's edition (Act Five, scene two, Bessel 1883), Dosifey's aria provides the audience with a much longer, secularized and

who was initially in agreement, refused to sing it. Thus the aria was simply omitted. See Vershinina, op. cit.

6. This reading of Musorgsky's original intent is not meant to denigrate Rimsky-Korsakov's remarkable achievement in crafting a performable version out of the *Khovanshchina* materials. Rimsky's was a very different musical and dramatic genius, but genius nevertheless. Where one must be on guard, it seems, is with Musorgsky's mentor and first biographer, Vladimir Stasov: aggressive propagandist in the cause of populist art, deeply necessary to Musorgsky as personal friend and ideological support, Stasov nevertheless often displayed terrible artistic taste and encouraged trivial lampoons at 'musical enemies' while remaining indifferent to technical subtlety. Much of what Musorgsky is believed to have disliked (Italian opera, operetta, Verdi, etc.) is in fact what Stasov disliked, and Stasov's advice on *Khovanshchina* was routinely poor. As their correspondence makes clear, Musorgsky respected Stasov, humoured him, gave in on the small things – but never on the big.

Joanna Borowska (Emma) and Vladimir Atlantov (Andrey) in the 1989 Vienna Staatsoper production (photo: Österreichischer Bundestheaterverband/Alex Zeininger)

business-like account of the opera's action to date. 'Brothers?' he sings. 'Our cause is lost! Throughout Russia we are persecuted. Old man Khovansky is dead, Golitsyn is in exile, our hope Prince Andrey is hiding with us in the hermitage. And whose fault is it? The quarrelling of the princes themselves . . . . The time has come to suffer for the Orthodox faith . . . We shall burn, but we shall not surrender!' In addition to recapitulating the essentials of this aspect of the plot, this stirring aria – in the spirit of Dosifey's most famous prototype, the great seventeenth-century Old Believer and martyr, the Archpriest Avvakum – delivers a stern moral verdict and warning to outsiders.

One could argue, however, that from a spiritual leader of the Old Belief on the very edge of transfiguration, such a politicized plot summary is completely out of character. For the boundary has already been crossed. To equate on the same plane the petty squabbling of those left behind with the dictates of divine destiny has the feel of blasphemy. In all likelihood, Dosifey, Marfa and their co-believers could no longer see or hear the fallen world. So the effect of Rimsky's trumpet fanfare at the end is invasive and profound. It aggressively returns the attention of the opera audience to secular history and its rights. The Old Belief, we are given to believe, has departed voluntarily into its 'afterworld on this earth', but we in the theatre still live in Petrine time; Peter's brass band is something that we, who share Peter's cosmos and legacy, can understand.

But try to imagine the effect of no Petrine time on stage at all. This is the effect of Stravinsky's final chorus, based on a melismatic Old Believer melody and marked at the end (as are all of Musorgsky's most devastating closures) *pianissimo*. Claudio Abbado adopted the Stravinsky ending for the first time since Diaghilev for the Vienna production in 1989. We should note how this transfer to 'Old Believer Time' is achieved. As the hermitage begins to burn, the actual ascent into it by a mass of swaying white-robed martyrs is increasingly stylized; under weirdly blue – not fiery – lights and vapour, a ritualized climbing by several draped figures culminates in a cobwebby tableau that is *frozen* in place.[7] By this time there is no more 'down below'. Marfa already sees wholly beyond earthly reality; accordingly, the world of her remembered experience can now be recoded as a dream. The key to this subtle threshold-crossing comes as Marfa sings to the terrified Andrey. 'My beloved! Remember that bright moment of love; since then I have dreamed many strange dreams, I dreamed that you had betrayed our love, and gloomy thoughts possessed me . . .' In this new context, Peter's trumpets, which sound beyond the forest, are merely a passing irritant. As the Old Believers gradually achieve their transition, these same trumpets will be perceived as heralds from a heavenly source.

What happens before our eyes is an absolute exit from our world. In the words of Stravinsky's psalm, 'God is my protector, He will not de-

---

7. I should note that my reading of the Vienna Opera's spectacular final scene is not entirely in the spirit of their own synopsis of it. Their account of Act Five reads: 'In death the Old Believers call on the Lord their Protector. The Petrinist troops arrive too late. The people are left alone, without leaders, without objectives, and without a future.' To which I would add: That is indeed the case as the final scene opens. But as immolation proceeds, the martyrs are not in death but 'in life', and perceive themselves as victors.

prive me of my faith.' The audience in the auditorium is watching the End of Time from the outside; the ones on stage have found the Russia they were seeking, whereas we have lost her. And thus is realized the utter *victory* of the Old Believer cause – not, as Rimsky would have it from his profane perspective in Dosifey's amended aria, its defeat. We are the ones walled out and left behind.

In his *Khovanshchina* Musorgsky left us a tantalizingly incomplete operatic vision. What might we expect from future revivals of *Khovanshchina* in the context of Russian culture? Throughout the 1980s and early 1990s, apocalypse enjoyed a special vogue among those confronting the ruins of the communist era. Both right- and left-wing thinkers, the disgusted ex-Marxists as well as ecologically-minded preservationists, were attracted by its maximalist historical hopelessness and by the challenge it offered to positivist materialism. In the words of one astute critic, 'the individual personal death of one person in his own bed is not seen as a problem worthy of attention: only death embodied in war or terror, i.e. only violent social death, attracts attention.' (B. Groys, 'Yes, Apocalypse, Yes, Now' (1987) in *Voprosy filosofii #3* , 1993.)

Perhaps ironically, however, apocalyptic thought promises enlightenment only to believers. And in the Russia of the post-communist period, it is precisely belief systems that have eroded. All who have lived through the 1980s and 1990s have been through the spiritual anxiety and sense of displacement that a secularized audience would feel in witnessing Stravinsky's final sacred chorus: the world as we know it is disappearing before our eyes, and in its place there is suddenly a whole other structure, alien, indifferent to *my* past, run by other principles. For better or worse, this was the deeply pessimistic vision that Musorgsky projected in his letter to Stasov during the Petrine Jubilee of 1872: 'The people groan, and drink to stifle their groans, and groan all the louder: we're still here!' Along what yet unknown paths and by what multiple faiths the Russian people will move forward in the twenty-first century, only one with the gifts of Musorgsky's Marfa will reveal.

THE ROMANOV DYNASTY
in the seventeenth century

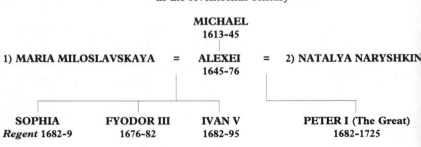

MICHAEL
1613-45

1) MARIA MILOSLAVSKAYA   =   ALEXEI   =   2) NATALYA NARYSHKIN
1645-76

SOPHIA   FYODOR III   IVAN V   PETER I (The Great)
Regent 1682-9   1676-82   1682-95   1682-1725

Musorgsky's New Music

Gerard McBurney

The first thing to understand about the drama and the music of *Khovanshchina* is that they are both different from the drama and the music of *Boris*. And this is odd because there still remain some similarities between the operas. The trouble is that it is these similarities (many of them tricks of detail and technique) that have had the unhappy effect of making us judge *Khovanshchina* too harshly against *Boris*, of hearing it as a falling-off from the earlier opera.

We miss certain things. We miss the endless dramatic surprises and twisting and turning of the Pretender's theme, we miss the melodic grandeur and heartfelt appeals to the audience in Boris's monologues. We miss the affectionate sweetness of the minor characters – the hostess, Varlaam, the nurse, the children. And we miss those emblematic figures of righteousness, Pimen and the Holy Fool. By contrast, everyone in *Khovanshchina*, even Dosifey and Marfa, seems tainted with collective guilt, untrustworthy. In *Boris*, the guilt had been so much easier to understand, lodged in the aching breast of a single man.

There is a quality of coldness in the characters of *Khovanshchina*. The music often feels almost callously designed to make us feel the great distance between them and us. In this respect, *Khovanshchina* may be seen to be quite different from the chamber-drama that was the first version of *Boris*, but still to have some very important points of connection with that key addition in the *second* version of *Boris*, the Polish Act. In the music of the Polish Act, as in the whole of *Khovanshchina*, the composer uses music not as a means of engaging our sympathies with the characters on stage, but as an instrument for the dissection and exposure of the living tissue of lies and deceit that joins the different characters together. The characters, that is to say, are no longer so important; the time drama is now located not within them, but between, around and beyond them. At times, Musorgsky seems almost to treat them as puppets.

Nonetheless, neither the music of the Polish Act nor of *Khovanshchina* is passionless. If the composer has turned cold towards his characters, he has certainly not turned cold towards the flood of the greater drama on the surface of which his almost helpless characters bob along. The problem is that his emotional attitude towards that flood is by no means so easy for us to understand and still less easy for us to accept. For what we loved about his earlier portrait about the tormented Boris was the pity of it. And now the pity seems to have ebbed away and a new note of cruelty and ruthlessness crept in. Now, instead of a single man looking backwards in despair and regretting a choice, a wrong choice he once made, we see and hear a whole historical process sweeping forwards inexorably (and with no room for choices) towards an unavoidable catastrophe. And the power and the danger of Musorgsky's music is such that, when the horror and the human squalor that it depicts have all been stripped away, it leaves us with the suggestion that for him, for the composer, there is

21

*Nicolai Ghiaurov as Ivan Khovansky in the 1989 Vienna Staatsoper production
(photo: Österreichischer Bundestheaterverband/Alex Zeininger)*

something wonderful and attractive, something thrilling and redemptive in the disaster that is to come.

Of course, Musorgsky was not the only person of his time and place who felt this way. This is an attitude and an assumption found lurking (and not always just lurking) in some of the greatest masterpieces of Russian literature written at the very time when Musorgsky was writing this music. And later, in the age of Scriabin and Blok, it was to become an obsession almost fatuously ubiquitous. But, as Richard Taruskin has shown us, as a point of view, it is certainly a far cry from the sentimental picture of a humane populist and a democrat. *Khovanshchina*, like *Prince Igor* and one or two other Russian operas, is sometimes described as a chronicle rather than a drama. (*Boris* is a drama, even a tragedy.) Now *Khovanshchina* is certainly not a real chronicle (it is not a good history) and the catastrophe towards which it leads is hardly undramatic. But what is true is that while in *Boris* the characters and the situation *evolve*, in *Khovanshchina*, they simply revolve, as though locked in some ghastly dance. No one, not Khovansky, Andrey, Marfa, Dosifey, Golitsyn, the Muscovites (known as New Arrivals or 'Prishliye lyudi'), the Old Believers, the Streltsy wives nor even the absent Peter is any different in character at the end (even if they are dead) from what they were at the beginning. Only the order has changed.

And something similar might be said to be true of the music. In *Boris*, the music constantly evolves and changes: the Pretender's theme, for instance, gathers ever greater significance to itself and changes its form to suit that new significance without, at the same time, losing its fundamental identity. We always recognise it when it comes back. In *Khovanshchina*, although ideas do return, they either return almost exactly the same, or the opposite, breaking and collapsing, as the order which they represent breaks and collapses around them.

This is a quality in the music of *Khovanshchina* which has disturbed later musicians. And perhaps this was why Rimsky-Korsakov and Shostakovich introduced their own elements of recapitulation in their (both) noble attempts to complete this uncompleted score. In particular they chose famously different solutions to the ending, both of them picking up suggestions from earlier music. And they operated something of the same principle at the end of Act Two (Rimsky-Korsakov even returns to the opera's prelude!), when Musorgsky himself had toyed with the astonishing idea of simply breaking off the dialogue with a single low unison note (an idea oddly reminiscent of Chekhov's sound of a snapping cable in *The Cherry Orchard*).

And Rimsky-Korsakov's manifold key changes and transpositions, these too seem motivated by much the same disturbed feeling, the urgent desire to introduce into the chaos of Musorgsky's world an ordered feel of ebb and flow, to provide moments of harmonic return to create balance and structure. The trouble is – and Shostakovich understood this very well – this was not the role which harmonic return played in Musorgsky's music. Identity of key was for him not an internal matter but an external one, frequently symbolic in effect and often tintinabulatory in character. When, in Musorgsky's music, we return to where we had been before, there is hardly ever a feeling of resolution and usually there is something almost of the opposite, a feeling of dissolution leading even to ecstasy. In other words, repetition for him was a matter of incantation.

What Musorgsky meant by recapitulation, repetition in *Khovansh-china*, how his special kind of incantation works in this opera, can be heard with peculiar power in the famous prelude, 'Dawn over the Moscow River'. Anyone who hears this music while at the same time holding in their head the music of the opening of *Boris Godunov*, will immediately be struck by the great change that has taken place in the composer's language – and that despite the fact that both pieces, as Taruskin tells us, are based on the same type of solo Russian folk-song, called the *protyazhnaya* (or 'melismatic song' as Taruskin evocatively translates it).

The music of the *Boris* opening is extraordinarily spare and massive, the different sections and devices of the *protyazhnaya* (precisely as Taruskin explains them) being laid out in Musorgsky's distinctively sombre orchestral manner with a laconic and analytical precision. Whether or not Musorgsky is actually quoting a real *protyazhnaya* is irrelevant; what he shows is a field-researcher's respect for the type of found material.

In *Khovanshchina*, things stand very differently. Even without the forbidden sweets of Rimsky-Korsakov ringing in our ears, this music is far lusher, more fluid and even more expansive. The melody is surrounded by nature-painting (bird-calls, the sun rising over the horizon) reaching out almost to Wagner, as well as the trumpet reveilles of the Streltsy and early-morning church bells that wickedly soften and make more commonplace the famous coronation bells from Boris.

But most fascinating is the detail of the treatment of the *protyazhnaya* melody itself. In his analysis of the genre, Taruskin points out that its melismatic freedom allows for an astonishing level of variation in the treatment of an individual melody, which, in turn, enables the singer to stray from someone else's version of the same song without ever quite losing the song's identity. It is this quality of the *protyazhnaya* which interests Musorgsky in the *Khovanshchina* prelude. Whereas, in the *Boris* opening, the tune had been something hard-edged and clearly defined (as well as being emblematic, an artifact of 'the folk'), here in *Khovanshchina* it has become something generalised and harder to grasp. The key quality of this kind of song that Musorgsky highlights here is the permutability of its small elements (its little motivic images and distinctive phrase endings). This enables him to keep reshuffling the bits of his tune so that although it is in fact different from what has gone before, it sounds almost the same and we accept the whole melodic line as a single unfolding tune (this is the opposite of classical variation where we accept as different something that is in fact the same). We also accept the tone-painting (the birds, trumpets and the rest) as part and parcel of the tune, for they are made from the same small bits (Russian musicologists nowadays would collect all these bits together and call them 'intonations').

There is a striking parallel here between this musical process in the prelude and the dramatic process of the whole opera. Both are, as it were, constructed from small bits which are constantly shuffled and reordered to create the illusion of a grand unfolding line. And in order to do this, Musorgsky must slightly lower our level of interest in the distinction of each little bit (whether a musical bit or a dramatic bit [i.e. a character in the story]), so as to lift our ears and minds away from the concrete detail

*E. Raikov as Golitsyn and Elena Obraztsova as Marfa with the Bolshoi
production on tour to La Scala (photo: E. Piccagliani)*

and out towards the epic sweep of the unfolding line of history. I have suggested that this helps to explain our lack of interest in the individual characters of this opera (especially by comparison with those of *Boris*). I would also suggest that the same, or something similar, applies to the music. And this is why we do not remember *Khovanshchina* for its tunes (again, especially by comparison with the wealth of memorable tunes in *Boris*). What matters about *Khovanshchina* is the unfolding of something longer than a tune.

But perhaps the key musical experience of *Khovanshchina* – and indeed one of the greatest scenes in nineteenth-century opera – is the Second Act, the scene in Golitsyn's study where the three main characters of the drama, Golitsyn, Khovansky and Dosifey, meet to discuss and vainly wrangle over their respective hierarchical positions in the historical process that swirls around them. Incidentally, it is a scene which has interesting parallels with some other great conversation-pieces from opera of that time, including the long confrontation between Philip II and the Grand Inquisitor in *Don Carlos* and some of Wotan's conversations with the female personages whom he has variously offended in the course of *The Ring* (significantly all these operatic conversations have caused difficulties for opera-goers down the years, depending as they do not on startling effects but on the precise meaning of what the characters are saying to one another). Apart from Golitsyn's servant, the only other figures who dare to intrude into the discussions in Golitsyn's study are the Lutheran pastor (representing the dark threat of the West far more interestingly than the diabolical Rangoni in *Boris*), Marfa (representing the supernatural power and moral authority of ancient Russia and the incontrovertible strength of the truth), and the boyar Shaklovity (the agent of political change against whom the three protagonists are united in hatred). These three intruders appear not together but in succession, to give names and a structure to the unfolding thoughts and conversations of Golitsyn, Khovansky and Dosifey.

It is worth pointing out the place of this Second Act in the structure of the whole opera. *Khovanshchina* has often been castigated as an almost incoherent muddle of events. In fact, it has a quite simple structure almost as pure and elegant as that which Taruskin has identified in the first version of *Boris*. Three scenes in the open air (Red Square, the Streltsy quarter beyond the river, Red Square again) frame two scenes in private apartments (Golitsyn's, Khovansky's). This five-part structure is then followed by a coda-apotheosis, the martyrdom of the Old Believers in the hermitage in the forest. Of the two scenes in private apartments, one, the Golitsyn scene, advances the action in words, the other, the Khovansky scene, in a single deed, the assassination.

It is in the musical word, the musical conversation, of Act Two that Musorgsky displays his greatest mastery and, indeed, his greatest originality as a composer and dramatist. It is here most of all that we can hear the new kind of music that, as he wrote excitedly in this letters to his friends, he found himself discovering at this time.

The question of musical speech had been at the centre of Musorgsky's attention since his earliest composition. Musorgsky's ideas on this subject were rooted not only in his friendship with the older Dargomyzhsky (who had for some time been experimenting with this sort of thing) but also in some of the wider and wilder propositions attempting to connect art and politics, that were current in Russia when Musorgsky was a young man. His most extreme attempt to join music to the realities of speech, his Gogol-inspired sketch, *The Marriage*, was left unfinished but it served nonetheless as the foundation upon which he built both his achievements in opera and his great output of songs.

But the language and technique of Musorgsky's word-setting did not stand still. And neither did his wider political and personal feelings, both of which are amply reflected in that very language and technique. When he wrote *The Marriage*, he was fascinated by the detailed rhythm and intonation of the language of ordinary people, treating it both as a comedy and as a manifestation of nature.

By the time he got to *Boris*, it was melody that was more interesting to him. What he found in that opera was an astonishing balance between the demands of melody as a way of setting the sound and meaning of words and the very different demands it made, both as a way of drawing us into sympathy with a character and as a way of pushing forward the drama.

I have already suggested that by the time he came to write *Khovanshchina*, Musorgsky was trying to expand beyond melody and character, to uncover the broader rise and fall of an unfolding process (musical and dramatic) against which a melody or a character would prove to be but one of a number of details. And the prelude demonstrates one way in which he does this. But Act Two shows him operating his new more expanded language on a far broader time-scale. And it is perhaps no surprise that this act should have been one of the parts of the opera that gave him most trouble, as well as being one of the passages most brutally chopped and transformed by Rimsky (who evidently considered it to be neither good music nor good drama).

The essence of the composer's language here lies in the way in which he unwinds from the spool of his imagination a single line, a line so strong that it proceeds for pages without much more than the barest harmonic support and is capable of being stopped and started all over again (all those modal cadences and sudden silences) without disturbing the feeling of inexorable flow. Indeed, in a paradoxical way, all those stops and starts actually increase the sense of unstoppable motion (and this is an essential point for the performer who must feel not only the progress of the notes, but the continuing progress behind the breaths and pauses).

When harmony emerges in this scene (in the supporting details and half-cadences and most of all in the divination scene with Marfa), it emerges *out* of melody and line, appearing as a momentary vertical expression of what remains a fundamental horizontal. Indeed, this music is probably the nearest that any nineteenth-century European musician ever approached to the Turkish music of the *mugham*, so familiar to travellers who visited the *caravanserais* on the Southern borders of the Russian empire. The *mugham*, like the Indian *raga*, is capable of almost infinite expansion. And the art of the musician in such cases lies at least in part in their ability to feel the possibility of endless continuity and expansion, always lurking beneath the local surface of the notes.

If I am right, and if indeed Musorgsky's music in this scene has some-

*Aage Haugland (Ivan Khovansky) and Martti Talvela (Dosifey) at the
Metropolitan Opera (photo: James Heffernan)*

thing of this quality, then I would suggest that this springs at least in part from his attempt to give expression to a quite new and alarming sense of time (new and alarming at least to a nineteenth-century musician). And if this is true, then maybe Musorgsky's failure to complete this piece was not only a result of alcoholic debilitude, but also the excruciating problem of finding a right way to bring an ending to a music and a drama that by no means necessarily demanded an ending.

Musorgsky, as music and words tell us in one of his most famous songs, and as we can hear in every note of *Khovanshchina*, was a composer, who had, like his character Marfa, seen a vision. And it may well be, as has often been observed, that behind the sad decline of his later years, there was, apart from the problems of his extra-musical life, also a general musical problem (not just in *Khovanshchina*): the problem of creating an ending. For the still young composer had chosen, with care and deliberation, to break the standard patterns of musical closure offered him by the Western tradition, and to look for a new kind of music, expressing, among other things, a new kind of time. And this had brought with it a whole range of problems which he was quite simply not in a position to solve (and nor was anyone else). And so his work remained endlessly unfinished.

It is perhaps for this reason as well as for others that we should have some sympathy for him, when, in writing this opera, he turned away from the warmer interest in individual human character that he showed in *Boris Godunov*, towards a more despairing and cynical vision of humanity, as well as to gaze longingly on an apocalyptic fire that he might indeed have hoped would bring certain things to an end.

The final scene in the 1971 performance at La Scala, Milan, designed by Nicola Benois in 1927, with Boris Christoff as Dosifey.

Helga Dernesch as Marfa and Martti Talvela as Dosifey at the Metropolitan Opera (photo: James Heffernan)

'Khovanshchina' in Context

Rosamund Bartlett

If the forces of Russian history were central to the subject matter of *Khovanshchina*, they were no less crucial to its composition. Until 1861, for example, one of Musorgsky's chief sources for the opera was considered so dangerous and inflammatory a document by the Russian government that its publication was expressly forbidden. The work in question might not seem an obvious candidate for censorship, for this was no scathing indictment of the Romanov dynasty penned by one of Musorgsky's contemporaries, but one of the masterpieces of old Russian literature: the autobiography of a deeply conservative seventeenth-century Orthodox priest. Its first draft completed exactly two centuries before Musorgsky started work on *Khovanshchina*, the Archpriest Avvakum's *Life Written by Himself* is a stirring account of the hardships and persecution endured by one of the leaders of the great Russian Church schism of 1666-67. (The schism was caused when Patriarch Nikon introduced reforms to the liturgy, which had deviated over time from the Greek model. These reforms were anathema to members of the Russian church who subscribed to the theory that Moscow was the 'Third Rome'.) In the eyes of the Tsarist government, however, Avvakum's heretical views represented more than just the voice of religious dissent. Ever since the Streltsy uprisings of 1682 (the events Musorgsky focuses on in *Khovanshchina*), the Old Believers had seemed to Russian officialdom to be linked inextricably to movements of popular rebellion, and Avvakum's autobiography was thus regarded as politically as well as theologically subversive. Although a few tentative steps were taken to remove the veil of secrecy that still surrounded the Old Believers and the history of the Schism in Nicholas I's last years as Tsar, it was only after the accession of Alexander II in 1855 that serious historical research into Russia's religious history began to be undertaken. Even in the new period of pre-revolutionary 'glasnost' which followed the stifling reaction and repression of Nicholas I's rule, Avvakum's autobiography only ceased to be the preserve of Old Believer 'samizdat' some six years later, when it was published by the literary scholar Nikolai Tikhonravov in 1861, the momentous year of the emancipation of the serfs.

It is no coincidence that many of the materials Musorgsky studied in preparation for the composition of his opera were first published after Nicholas I's death; in this respect, *Khovanshchina* is a true product of its age. It is certainly important to bear in mind that the thirty-three-old composer approached the Streltsy rebellions with none of the hindsight afforded by access to a full range of published documents on the subject. Russian scholarship on the late seventeenth century was still in its infancy when Musorgsky began to write the libretto to his opera, and the historical works he was able to consult were not always objective. The temporary relaxation of the censorship that came with the period of

Donald McIntyre (Shaklovity) and David Ward (Khovansky) at Covent Garden,
(photo: Reg Wilson)

Alexander II's Great Reforms, however, meant that much valuable archival material could now be consulted and published, and it also became possible to challenge the official viewpoint on historical events. A crucial figure in this regard, with a pivotal (if invisible) role in *Khovanshchina*, is the illustrious personality of Peter the Great.

The founder of imperial Russia's capital city was not only in people's minds in the late 1860s and early 1870s because Alexander II was optimistically (and mistakenly, as it turned out) hailed by the reform-minded as a 'new' Peter. The year in which Musorgsky began *Khovanshchina* may have marked two centuries since Avvakum completed the first draft of his autobiography, but it was also the bicentenary year of the birth of the tsar the Old Believers had come to perceive as the Antichrist. Despite the proliferation of lavish celebrations and official eulogies to the man who, it was generally believed, had single-handedly created the modern Russian state, there had been something of a sea-change in attitudes towards Peter and his reforms since the 1830s, when the cult of his personality (actively encouraged by Nicholas I's doctrine of official nationality) was at its peak, and his image was that of a 'demiurge creating being from nonbeing'. Since Karamzin's *History of the Russian State* (then the only reliable history of Russia) stopped at the beginning of the seventeenth century, a key source of inspiration for the historical novels that became fashionable in the 1830s were the thirty highly laudatory volumes of the *Deeds of Peter the Great, Wise Reformer of Russia* (published between 1782 and 1801), compiled by the amateur historian Ivan Golikov. Although the authorities continued to extol Peter and his achievements throughout and following Nicholas I's reign, some (including Musorgsky) had begun to take a more ambivalent view, even if Golikov's *Deeds of Peter the Great* appears prominently in the list of publications he read for *Khovanshchina*. But while an interest in Peter the Great was not particularly unusual among Russian artists and writers in the 1870s (Tolstoy, for example, spent the whole of 1872 collecting materials for a novel about Peter the Great before abandoning it to write *Anna Karenina*), using the chaotic events leading up to Peter's accession and the Russian church schism as creative material certainly was. Here Musorgsky was a pioneer, for these were subjects which would later inspire a miniature renaissance in the genre of the historical novel (including a novel about the schism by Musorgsky's acquaintance Daniil Mordovtsev), as well as a host of other artistic, literary and musical works by artists such as Surikov, Repin, Leskov, and Rimsky-Korsakov.

Given that Musorgsky had to construct his text largely with the aid of primary sources, it is hardly surprising that he found his project at times overwhelming, particularly in view of his methodical concern for authenticity. He was, after all, tackling a subject that only now was beginning to receive attention from scholars and writers, and did not have the advantage of working with a ready-made text, as he had done with Pushkin's *Boris Godunov*. Even as late as 1863-64, there were very few studies of the century available at all, because previous histories generally only covered events up until the beginning of the Romanov dynasty. Then, however, the volumes about Sophia's regency appeared in Sergei Soloviev's *History of Russia*, a magisterial publication which Musorgsky knew well. As the first exclusive study of the last decades of the seventeenth century, Peter

Shchebalsky's *The Regency of Tsarevna Sophia*, published in 1856, was therefore an important item in the list of reading materials Musorgsky consulted at the St Petersburg Public Library, particularly in view of its comparative objectivity when set against such monuments of hagiography as Golikov's *magnum opus*. Also useful were the portraits of Sophia and Prince Golitsyn, published in the journal *Russkoe slovo* in 1859, by the writer Mikhail Semevsky, whose attitude towards Peter I, incidentally, was extremely hostile. Nikolai Ustrialov's *History of the Reign of Peter the Great*, which dealt with the years of Sophia's regency to some degree, and was published two years later, was more detailed and scholarly in its approach. Interestingly, Musorgsky did not include it in the bibliography which he presented to Stasov in July 1872, which was made up of a mixture of contemporary memoirs and nineteenth-century interpretations of events, perhaps because his book was officially commissioned. Like most historians of the epoch, Ustrialov is highly critical of Sophia's administration, partly for misogynistic reasons, partly because of the ever-flourishing Petrine cult. Perusal of the twelve pages of notes that Musorgsky made in preparation for his libretto and the letters he wrote to Stasov at the time, however, makes it clear that neither Sophia nor Peter constituted the chief focus of his interest; the 1682 Streltsy rebellion and the schism seem to have been what captivated his imagination above all.

Musorgsky was fortunate that towards the end of the seventeenth century, individual memoirs began to replace the anonymous chronicles, hitherto compiled by monks, which gave him the opportunity to form a reasonably balanced view of the period. Among the principal eye-witness accounts of the Streltsy rebellions were the journals of the westerniser and diplomat Count Andrei Matveev, which contain a detailed – and heavily partisan – account of the 1682 Streltsy rebellion (which he had witnessed as a teenager), the diaries of fellow diplomat and government official Ivan Zhelyabuzhsky, which contain much valuable material on the 1698 uprising, and a memoir written by the monk Silvester Medvedev, whose arguments in favour of Sophia provide a refreshing corrective amongst a sea of pro-Petrine views. It was perhaps the extreme panegyrical tone of a memoir of Peter by Petr Krekshin, a nobleman from Novgorod, that made Musorgsky decide not to include it in his list of materials consulted, despite the fact that he mentions having studied it in a letter to Stasov.

The Archpriest Avvakum's remarkable autobiography naturally formed the centrepiece in Musorgsky's reading about the schism. Like successive generations of Russian writers, from Tolstoy to Solzhenitsyn, Musorgsky was clearly enchanted by the passion and humour of Avvakum's writing, by his masterful and unprecedented use of vernacular Russian (at a time when Church Slavonic was still used as the literary language), and by his great gifts as a storyteller. Other, less entertaining but equally important, works on the schism which Musorgsky devoured include Ivan Filippov's *History of the Vygovsk Old Believers Monastery*, published in 1862, which describes life at one of the first Old Believer communities, and the various items published in Tikhonravov's *Annals of Russian Literature and Antiquity*, one of which (concerning the birth of Peter, the 'Antichrist') he recounts with great relish in a letter to Stasov.

The final scene in a production in Poznan (photo: courtesy of Opera Magazine)
and at Covent Garden, designed in 1963 by Bozidar Rašica and directed by
Vlado Habuneck (photo: Donald Southern)

Proof that Musorgsky's interest in the schism went beyond collecting materials for *Khovanshchina* is provided by the fact that he had started reading about it even before he began work on the opera. In 1870, for example, he wrote to thank his friend, the historian Vladimir Nikolsky, for lending him Filippov's work on the Vygovsk monastery, and Ivan Troitsky's *History of the Schism*. As Soviet scholars have shown, Musorgsky also drew much from the Populist historian Afanasy Shchapov's important book on the schism, which was published in 1859. Another prominent Populist historian who also argued that there was a progressive social element to the rebellion of those who were determined to cling stubbornly to the traditions of old Muscovy was Nikolai Kostomarov, who published an article on the subject in 1870. Since Kostomarov happened to be a personal friend of Musorgsky, it may safely be assumed that the composer read and discussed this article with its author at some point during the composition of *Khovanshchina*. The fact that in an autobiographical note of 1880 Musorgsky acknowledges the assistance of Kostomarov, as well as that of Nikolsky, in the planning of the opera further suggests that he may have also been sympathetic to his views. In espousing the view that the people rather than rulers were the true subject for historians, Kostomarov's approach in many ways ran counter to that of Soloviev, whose focus was primarily on those who governed.

That Musorgsky's interest in his nation's history and destiny was profound and all-absorbing is beyond a doubt. 'History is my nocturnal friend', he wrote to Vladimir Stasov in September 1873; 'it brings me pleasure and intoxication.' Trying to fathom an overall purpose in the way Musorgsky uses Russian history in *Khovanshchina* will always remain difficult, however, and not only because he left the work unfinished at his death. Musorgsky was partly drawn to the period of the Streltsy troubles because he saw parallels with the turbulent times in which he himself lived. 'The past within the present' is what he proclaimed as his task in a much-quoted letter to Stasov, who had first suggested to him the idea of writing an opera on the Streltsy rebellions. By this Musorgsky meant to imply that the thin patina of Western civilisation introduced by Peter the Great obscured an awful truth: that the vast majority of the Russian population was essentially still in the dark ages; 'We're still here!' he repeats four times, the word 'here' meaning presumably the time period of the Khovansky disturbances. By writing an opera about the conflicts and struggles of late seventeenth-century Russia, in which neither the populace nor their leaders ultimately have any control over events, Musorgsky thus hoped, it seems, to show how illusory and erroneous the concept of historical progress was where Russia was concerned. A century later, the opera has lost none of its relevance with the Russian people once again facing an uncertain destiny following the demise of Soviet power. Divining 'the present within the past' may also have been in Musorgsky's mind. With the acute sensitivity of a great artist, he also seems in his opera to be predicting the impending breakdown of the old order, which would bring with it the end of Imperial Russia. By the end of the 1870s, after all, the Populists' peaceful attempts to convert the peasantry to socialism had already given way to terrorism, which would result in the assassination of Alexander II, three days before Musorgsky's own death, in 1881. *Khovanshchina* is thus in some respects an eloquent counterpart to the great novels of the period, *Anna Karenina* and *The Brothers Karamazov* (both of which were written in the 1870s), which mirror the spiritual crisis and moral and social chaos of late nineteenth-century European culture.

Musorgsky began his career as an elegant dilettante in the Preobrazhensky guards, the elite regiment founded by Peter the Great, which is featured in *Khovanshchina*. But as what exactly did he end his life? Was he the radical Populist whom successive generations of Soviet critics have identified, or did he remain ultimately an aristocrat? Is *Khovanshchina* chiefly about the battle between the 'old' Russia and the 'new' Russia as Stasov claims, an apologia for Peter the Great's reforms, or is it a drama of the Russian people? Is it a religious tragedy or an aristocratic tragedy? Or is there an element of plausibility in all these interpretations? The preponderance of main characters from the nobility does indeed make it difficult to argue that *Khovanshchina* was inspired by Populist ideas, yet we know that Musorgsky was next planning to write an opera about the Pugachev uprising, using Pushkin's story *The Captain's Daughter*, which would complete his trilogy of operas about Russian rebellions. Pugachev was certainly no nobleman. The ambiguous and undeniably bleak ending of *Khovanshchina* seems to demonstrate that Musorgsky's sympathies lie neither with the forces of 'old' Muscovy nor with those of the 'new' state coming into being, but rather with Mother Russia herself, who emerges as the opera's only true tragic heroine. Musorgsky's early biographer M. D. Calvocoressi was thus not all that far from the mark in claiming that 'the drama is one, not of persons, but of a nation – of Russia, torn by conflicting tendencies and confronted with an unknown future'. As such, *Khovanshchina* fits admirably into the artistic tradition of a country whose people know, and understand better than most, suffering and sacrifice, a tradition in which weakness and failure are often valued higher than power and strength. The lament for the sad destiny of Russia, oppressed by her own people, is first struck up by the chorus of Muscovites in Act One, then returns as a refrain, to be voiced by each of the protagonists in turn over the course of the work. 'In Russia we love the losers', Tatyana Tolstaya has written, in explaining the complicated feelings her people have for Boris Yeltsin. In certain important respects, it is the same love which informs Tolstoy's sympathy for the doomed Anna Karenina, and Dostoevsky's compassion for the sinner Dmitri Karamazov, in the two great novels written while this great historical opera was being composed, that permeates Musorgsky's sentiments about Russia's destiny in *Khovanshchina*.

Thematic Guide

These brief musical themes are numbered in square brackets which refer
to the libretto.

[1] Dawn over Moscow

Andante tranquillo

[2] Kuzka

Moderato, non troppo lento

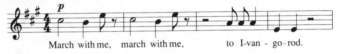

March with me, march with me, to I-van-go-rod.

[3] The Scribe

Moderato

[4] Streltsy

[5] Muscovites

Largo, ma non troppo

Our be-lov-ed __ home - land so dear.

[6] Ivan Khovansky

Moderato assai, quasi marziale

cresc.

[7] Emma

Con allegrezza. capriccioso e sempre agitato

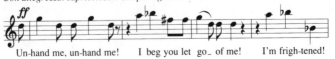

Un-hand me, un-hand me! I beg you let go_ of me! I'm frigh-tened!

[8] Prince Andrey Khovansky

No, _ no, the tur - tle dove can - not es - cape from the fal-con!

[9] Marfa

Adagio cantabile

Thus, oh _ prince, thou pre - serv - est thy con-stan-cy!

[10] Dosifey

Andante non troppo. Doloroso

The time is _ nigh when dark-ness in - vades our earth-ly _ spi - rits

[11] Old Believers

Meno mosso, mistico

Fa - ther save our souls from the path of _ he - re-sy. _

[12] Golitsyn

Andante cantabile. Con delicatezza

[13] Marfa's mystic music

[14] Marfa describes Golitsyn's exile

A tempo, tranquillo

[15] Ivan Khovansky

We no long - er know our pla - - ces.

[16] Old Believers

Moderato non troppo. Pomposo

True _ be - liev - ers __ join as bro-thers

[17] Marfa

Andantino non troppo, cantabile

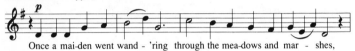

Once a mai-den went wand - 'ring through the mea-dows and mar - shes,

[18] Marfa

Andante appassionato

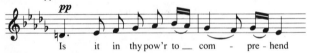

Is it in thy pow'r to _ com - pre - hend

[19] Susanna

Moderato

Thou art de - ceiv - ing me.

[20] Shaklovity

Ah, I des - pair at your suf-fer-ing, Rus - sia my home-land.

[21] Streltsy men

Moderato energico

40

[22] Streltsy women

Alla breve

Oh, you dis - gust - ing, stink - ing drunk - ards!

[23] Kuzka

Allegro scherzando

Ga-ther round to hear the tel -ling of a wo-man who was dwell-ing

[24] The Dance of the Persian Slave Girls

Andante cantando con espressione

[25] The Song of the White Swan

Andantino

The swan was swim - ming si -lent-ly, la - du, la - du. __

[26] The Preobrazhensky March

legato

[27] The Hymn of the Old Believers

Andante maestoso, alla breve

Oh __ God __ our re - deem - er __

41

Streshnev, Tsar Peter's herald, announces the pardon of the Streltsy at the Kirov, Leningrad, 1960

Evgeny Nesterenko as Khovansky surrounded by his Persian dancing girls at Covent Garden, 1982 (photo: Clive Barda)

KHOVANSHCHINA
THE KHOVANSKY AFFAIR

A National Music Drama

M. P. MUSORGSKY
English Translation by Carol Borah Palca

Khovanshchina was first performed on February 21 1886 in the version by Rimsky-Korsakov in the Amateur Musical-Dramatic Club, St Petersburg. The first major production was at the Maryinsky Theatre, St Petersburg, on November 7 1911.

The first performance of the Stravinsky final chorus, and the orchestration by Ravel, was on June 5 1913 at the Théâtre des Champs-Elysées, Paris. The first performance in London was at the Theatre Royal, Drury Lane, on July 1 1913. The first performance in the USA was in Philadelphia on April 18 1928.

The first staged performance of the Shostakovich version was on November 25 1960 at the Kirov Theatre, Leningrad.

*

This translation was commissioned by English National Opera for the first production of the opera at the London Coliseum in November 1994. Particular attention was given to the curious manner of speech of different characters, none of whom speak in everyday Russian; in particular we sought to express the antique diction of the Old Believers. Many amendments have inevitably been made in rehearsal, after this text went to press.

The Russian text was prepared by Catriona Bass from the Lamm/Shostakovich vocal score, and she also translated the stage directions.

Although Musorgsky conceived the opera in 1872, he did not write out his libretto in the 'blue notebook' until 1879. He entitled the libretto 'Opera in Six Scenes'. The division of the opera into five acts was made by Rimsky-Korsakov. Richard Taruskin, writing in the New Grove Dictionary of Opera (1992), surmises that the fair copy of the text in the blue notebook may have been made for the submission to the censor. He further writes that the second scene (ie Act Two) was unfinished and the last scene (ie Act Five) was 'little more than a sheaf of sketches'. Musorgsky's fair copy is almost entirely in prose, only giving the songs in verse. At certain points it seemed to us that the text was easier to read broken into verse, and we have set out these passages accordingly. Where it varies from the text in the vocal score, we have followed the latter.

KHOVANSHCHINA
THE KHOVANSKY AFFAIR

THE CHARACTERS

Prince Ivan Khovansky *the leader of the Streltsy*	*bass*
Prince Andrey Khovansky *his son*	*tenor*
Prince Vasily Golitsyn	*tenor*
Shaklovity a *Boyar*	*baritone*
Dosifey *the leader of the Old Believers*	*bass*
Marfa *an Old Believer*	*contralto*
Susanna *an elderly Old Believer*	*soprano*
Scribe	*tenor*
Emma *a girl from the German quarter*	*soprano*
Pastor	*bass*
Varsonofiev *Golitsyn's confidant*	*bass*
Kuzka *a Streltsy soldier*	*tenor*
Streshnev *a Boyar*	*tenor*
1st Soldier	*bass*
2nd Soldier	*bass*
Attendant on Golitsyn	*tenor*

Muscovites, Old Believers, Streltsy, Streltsy women, Peasant girls and Persian slaves belonging to Ivan Khovansky, soldiers of Tsar Peter's Poteshny regiment, People.

ХОВАНЩИНА
Народная музыкальная драма

Музыка
М.П. МУСОРГСКОГО

ДЕЙСТВУЮЩИЕ ЛИЦА

Князь Иван Хованский *вождь стрельцов*	*бас*
Князь Андрей Хованский *его сын*	*тенор*
Князь Василий Голицын	*тенор*
Шакловитый *боярин*	*баритон*
Досифей *глава раскольников*	*бас*
Марфа *раскольница*	*контральто*
Сусанна *старая раскольница*	*сопрано*
Подьячий	*тенор*
Эмма *девушка из Немецкой слободы*	*сопрано*
Пастор	*бас*
Варсонофьев *приближенный Голицына*	*бас*
Кузька *стрелец*	*баритон*
Стрешнев *боярин*	*тенор*
1-й Стрелец	*бас*
2-й Стрелец	*бас*
Клеврет Князя Голицыына	*тенор*

Московские пришлые люди, раскольники, стрельцы, стрелецкие жены, сенные девушки и персидские рабыни Ивана Хованского, петровские "потешные", народ.

ACT ONE

[1] *Moscow. Red Square. A stone pillar with inscribed copper tablets mounted on it. On the right is the Scribe's booth. Guard chains are stretched across the square. It is dawn. A Streltsy sentry is at the pillar. The curtain rises slowly. The stage is bathed in early morning light. The sun lights up the steeples of the churches. The bells ring for the morning service. Gradually the whole stage lights up as the sun rises. Streltsy trumpets are heard offstage. Kuzka is lying by the pillar.*

KUZKA
(half-asleep)

[2]
March with me, march with me...
To Ivangorod...
I'll smash in, I'll smash in...
All their doors and windows...
(*A Streltsy patrol enters and removes the chains.*)
I'll capture, I'll capture...
A lovely maiden...

2nd SOLDIER

Hear him snoring!

1st SOLDIER

So? Let him be Antipich, you know we did a good night's work.

2nd SOLDIER

You're telling me!

1st SOLDIER

That old clerk of the council Larivon Ivanov had his whole chest slashed open with a hatchet.

2nd SOLDIER

And then that German boy, the one we found around the church yard, screaming as we dragged him here, so we tore him quickly into pieces.

Offstage trumpets

1st SOLDIER

What a racket!

KUZKA
(half-asleep)

Oh, do not shake, do not shake me...
Rock me.
Ah, do not strike, do not strike me...
Cradle me.

2nd SOLDIER

When they protect the baby Tsars from their enemies, can't they do it more discreetly?

1st SOLDIER

They're bastards every one, the Boyar scoundrels, thieving and plundering, they rob the treasury.

Offstage trumpets

2nd SOLDIER

The chief's awake now.

KUZKA
(jumping up)

Hey, get out of here! I'll show them!

1st and 2nd SOLDIERS

What a sentry on the look-out, never sleeping, well done, Kuzka!

KUZKA

To hell with both of you!

1st SOLDIER

Poor little pup, can't get it up!

48

ДЕЙСТВИЕ ПЕРВОЕ

Москва. Красная площадь. Каменный столб и на нем медные доски с надписями. Справа будка подьячего. Наискось площади на столбах протянуты сторожевые цепи. Светает. Главы церквей освещаются восходящим солнцем. Доносится благовест к заутрене. Вся сцена постепенно освещается восходящим солнцем. Слышны звуки вестовых стрелецких труб. У столба спит сторожевой стрелец Кузька.

КУЗЬКА
(сквозь дремоту)

Подойду, подойду...
Под Иван-город...
Вышибу, вышибу...
Каменны... стены...
(На площадь входит стрелецкий дозор - 1-й и 2-й стрельцы. Они снимают цепи.)
Выведу, выведу...
Красную девицу...

2-Й СТРЕЛЕЦ

Вона, дрыхнет !

1-Й СТРЕЛЕЦ

Эх, ништо, брат Антипыч! Вчера не мало потрудились.

2-Й СТРЕЛЕЦ

Что говорить...

1-Й СТРЕЛЕЦ

Как дьяку-то думному, Ларивону Иванову, грудь раздвоили камнем вострым...

2-Й СТРЕЛЕЦ

А немца Гадена у Спаса на Бору имали, а и сволокли до места и ту по членам разобрали.

Трубы

1-Й СТРЕЛЕЦ

Вот так рявкают !

КУЗЬКА
(сквозь дремоту)

Ох, не колышь меня...
Буйный ветер.
Ох, не подкось мои
Ноженьки...

2-СТРЕЛЕЦ

Во имя божье сохраняют немолочно жизнь и здравие царей младых.

1-СТРЕЛЕЦ

От недругов лихих, бояр спесивых, лихоимателей, казны грабителей.

Трубы

2-СТРЕЛЕЦ

"Верх" поднялся.

КУЗЬКА
(вскакивая)

Где грабители? Вот я им !

1-Й И 2-Й СТРЕЛЬЦЫ

Ай да Кузька, стражник знатный, ай да паря, право любо !

КУЗЬКА

Да что вы, дьяволы.

1-Й СТРЕЛЕЦ

Ох, ты стрелец, худой конец.

2-Й СТРЕЛЕЦ

Воевода, взгромаздился на урода. Ха, ха, ха...

2nd SOLDIER

He knows his station: only sleeps with close relations. Ha, ha, ha, ha...

KUZKA
(teasing)

Poor little pup, can't get it up! Ha, ha, ha...To hell with you. It's still the middle of the night.

1st and 2nd SOLDIERS

The middle of the night! Early services are over. And look there, see the scribe at work.

[3]   *The scribe enters, and goes up to his booth, sharpening his quill.*

1st SOLDIER

Feather-scratcher!

KUZKA

There's ink on him from head to toe!

2nd SOLDIER

All chicken scratches!

They approach the scribe.

1st and 2nd SOLDIERS

Honourable majesty of wisdom.

They bow.

KUZKA

Ascend your royal throne here on this post. Ha, ha, ha...

1st and 2nd SOLDIERS

Ha, ha, ha...

They go off to the Kremlin.

SCRIBE
(rubbing his hands)

It's Sodom and Gomorrah! What times these are! Horrible! But money can be made. Yes!

Shaklovity enters and goes up to the booth.

SHAKLOVITY

Hey! Hey you, you scribbler! I've come to you guided by the grace of God.

SCRIBE

Thank you most kindly, gracious, noble sir. How you honour this unworthy, lowly servant. I do not deserve your kindness.

SHAKLOVITY

Right then, never mind, just listen: I've most important work for you.

SCRIBE

Right, fine. I can do it,
only takes a moment.
I am clever, neat and orderly;
accusations are my speciality.

SHAKLOVITY

If you can face the torture chamber,
if the torments of the rack do not frighten you,
if you are willing to renounce your family,
forget all the things you hold most dear,
then write!

SCRIBE

God above!

SHAKLOVITY

But, if we ever chance to meet again one day and you reveal who I am only God above can help you then. Get it?

SCRIBE

Listen: can't you find another scribbler, gracious, noble sir? That's some bargain that you are offering. Thanks just the same.

КУЗЬКА
(передразнивая их)

Ох ты, стрелец, худой конец... Ха-ха-ха-ха...Ну... кой черт вас по ночам здесь носит?

1-Й И 2-Й СТРЕЛЬЦЫ

Какое по ночам! Уж и утрени отбыли. Гляди-кось: сам строчила прет.

К будке приближается подьячий,на ходу очинивая перо.

1-Й СТРЕЛЕЦ

Гуся точит.

КУЗЬКА

Чернилище-то, господи!

2-Й СТРЕЛЕЦ

Вот заскрыпит-то !

Подходят к подьячему.

1-Й И 2-Й СТРЕЛЬЦЫ

Вашему приказному степенству...

Кланяются.

КУЗЬКА

Скорей на этот столбик угодить! Ха-ха-ха...

1-Й И 2-Й СТРЕЛЬЦЫ

Ха-ха-ха...

Стрельцы, смеясь, уходят к Кремлю.

ПОДЬЯЧИЙ
(Потирая руки.)

Содома и Гоморра! Вот времечко! Тяжкое! А все ж прибыток справим... Да!

К будке подьячего подходит Шакловитый.

ШАКЛОВИТЫЙ

Эй!.. Эй, ты! Строчило! Со мною бог милости тебе прислал.

ПОДЬЯЧИЙ

Благодарим, добрый человек. А яз грешный, недостойный раб божий, не сподобился зрети.

ШАКЛОВИТЫЙ

Дадно, не в том дело. Смекни-ко: заказец важный есть тебе.

ПОДЬЯЧИЙ

Что ж! Что ж, настрочим,
мигом настрочим.
По уряду, по укладу
настрочим доносец лихо.

ШАКЛОВИТЫЙ

Если можешь пытку стерпеть,
если дыбы и застенок не страшат тебя,
если ты можешь от семьи отречься,
забыть все, что дорого тебе...
строчи!

ПОДЬЯЧИЙ

Господи!

ШАКЛОВИТЫЙ

Но, ежели когда-нибудь, при встрече со мной, ты выдашь меня, – оборони тебя господь тогда! Помни!

ПОДЬЯЧИЙ

Знаешь, проходи-ко ты мимо, добрый человек; больно много посулил ты, друг мой любезный.

ШАКЛОВИТЫЙ

Строчи, живо!

SHAKLOVITY

Just write, damn you!

SCRIBE
(peevishly)
Well then! You're getting on my nerves. Oh go away!

SHAKLOVITY
(laying a purse on the table)
Just write!

The scribe goes for the purse, rubbing his hands.

SCRIBE
(obsequiously)
Ah, I've changed my mind, my friend. You shall see, I give satisfaction, I'm your man!

SHAKLOVITY
'To you, great and mighty noble Tsars of our land, and to the Princes who, with wisdom, oversee the governance of Mother Russia.'
(The scribe writes.)
Is that clear?

SCRIBE
Don't worry, it's all clear, sir. Get on with it.

SHAKLOVITY
'Information has been received in secret from the Moscow Streltsy that Ivan Khovansky, the Boyar, and his son, Prince Andrey, are planning to incite dissension and rebellion.'

SCRIBE
(writing)
He's really lost his mind! Wealth has turned his head!

SHAKLOVITY
Let's hear it!

A small group of Muscovites' cross the square, singing.

MUSCOVITES
(offstage)
Master Koom and Mistress Kooma,
Missed her Koom and Koom missed Kooma.
Koom and Mistress Kooma heard a rumour,
Did Miss Koomer kiss the roomer?
'Roomer kissed Miss Kooma,' went the rumour.
'Roomer missed Miss Kooma,' said Mistress Kooma.
'No more roomer,' said Miss Kooma!

SCRIBE
(reading)
'To you, great and mighty noble Tsars of our land, and to the Princes who, with wisdom, oversee the governance of Mother Russia. Information has been received in secret from the Moscow Streltsy that Ivan Khovansky, the Boyar, and his son, Prince Andrey, are planning to incite dissension and rebellion.'

SHAKLOVITY
Very good. Copy some more. 'They have called upon all their comrades – traitors eager to join their scheming, to infiltrate society in Moscow, to hold their secret meetings to urge the people to assassinate the Boyars. *(The scribe writes.)* And then to instigate an insurrection throughout the land in every single province. They conspire to cause the landed peasants to rise against their own provincial leaders, creating turmoil and unrest so they might seize judicial power for those Old Believers among us, and to place on the throne of Moscow, Prince Andrey Khovansky...'

STRELTSY
(offstage)
Hey, move it!

SCRIBE
(crying out)
I'm dead and done for no one can save me. They'll know my writing. I won't be pardoned.

ПОДЬЯЧИЙ
(сварливо)

Вишь ты! Да дуй тебя горой!.. Отчаливай!

ШАКЛОВИТЫЙ
(кладя на стойку кошель)

Строчи.

Подьячий, посягая на кошель, потирает руки.

ПОДЬЯЧИЙ
(сладкоречиво)

А!.. Ну, сказывай. У нас, брат, комар носа не подточит…
Сказывай!

ШАКЛОВИТЫЙ

"Царям-Государям и Великим Князьям всеа Великия, и Малыя, и Белыя России
Самодержцам…"

(Подьячий пишет.)

Настрочил?

ПОДЬЯЧИЙ

Уж ты не сумлевайся… знай сказывай.

ШАКЛОВИТЫЙ

…Извещают московские стрелец люди на Хованских: боярина Князь Ивана да
сына его Андрея; замутить хотят на государстве.

ПОДЬЯЧИЙ
(пишет)

Не солоно хлебал! С жиру бесится.

ШАКЛОВИТЫЙ

Прочти-ко !

Небольшая группа московского люда проходит с песней через площадь.

МОСКОВСКИЕ ПРИШЛЫЕ ЛЮДИ
(за сценой)

Жила кума, была кума
кума кума увидала
кума кума не признала
Сидит кума, глядит кума
Куме кум кум деньги сулит,
куме кум куме рубль дарит
кума деньгу за пазуху.

ПОДЬЯЧИЙ
(читает)

"Царям-Государям и Великим Князьям всеа Великия, и Малыя, и Белыя России
Самодержцам, извещают московские стрелец люди на Хованских: боярина
Князь Ивана да сына его Андрея; замутить грозят на государстве."

ШАКЛОВИТЫЙ

Верно. Дальше строчи. "Звали на помочь свою братию, как бы царство им
доступити. А для того изневесть в город прийти большим собранием, народ
смущать, чтоб много больших бояр побил, *(Подьячий пишет.)* а там мутить по
всей Руси великой, по деревням, по селам, и посадам, делом злым на воевод, на
власти поднять с тягла честное хрестьянство. А станет смута на Руси, в тот раз
избрать властей надежных, чтоб старые книги любили, а на царстве Московском
сесть Хованскому Андрею…"

СТРЕЛЬЦЫ
(вдали)

Гой, лихо!

ПОДЬЯЧИЙ
(вскрикивает)

Ай! Прямая погибель, не будет пошады! Князь все узнает, князь не простит
мне…

53

STRELTSY
(offstage)

Hey, go on there!

SCRIBE

God above! They'll make me suffer, whip me and beat me until I die from torture.

[4]   STRELTSY
Stand aside for soldiers,
Streltsy soldiers.
Tough fighters.
We take pleasure, take our pleasure in the fight.

SHAKLOVITY
(anxiously)

The Streltsy...
Hear them?

He pulls his coat around him and hides behind the pillar.

SCRIBE
(quickly hiding the letter)

Oh, Mama, I'm terrified!

STRELTSY

No one ever can defeat us,
We are hard and daring.
We take pleasure,
Take pleasure in the fight.
We slaughter any son or daughter
Who defies us.

SHAKLOVITY
(going up to the scribe's booth)

They're passing. Listen, you scribbler!

SCRIBE
(frightened)

Be quiet!

SHAKLOVITY

Now listen to me!

Shaklovity ponders the denunciation. The scribe pulls out the letter and corrects it.

SCRIBE
(listening, calming down)

Glory be to God above! They've passed without stopping. I can't begin to tell you how I hate those villains. They're not human! Wild savage creatures! Everything they touch ends in death and bloody disaster, a trail of cries and weeping. Just doing their job, keeping law and order.

SHAKLOVITY

Listen! Quickly finish it up! 'At present we must remain in hiding. But when God sees fit to bring peace across our country, we shall reveal ourselves.'

SCRIBE
(writing)

'Remain in hiding...' 'reveal ourselves...' *(to Shaklovity)* It's finished.

SHAKLOVITY

'To the Tsarevna.'

SCRIBE
(writing)

'To the Tsarevna.'

SHAKLOVITY
(taking the letter)

May God have mercy on your soul. Watch out I warn you.

SCRIBE

I've had enough of your warnings and tough talking. You're just a puffed-up braggard, a crowing, cackling rooster! You've got some money, so you bully us.

СТРЕЛЬЦЫ
(вдали)

Гой вы, люди!

ПОДЬЯЧИЙ

Пыткой жестокой, плетью в застенке замучат до смерти!

СТРЕЛЬЦЫ

Гой вы, люди ратные,
Вы, стрельцы удалые,
Гой, гуляйте,
Вы гуляйте весело!

ШАКЛОВИТЫЙ
(тревожно)

Стрельцы!..
Слышишь?

Закрывается охабнем и отходит к столбу.

ПОДЬЯЧИЙ
(торопливо пряча письмо)

Ой, матушки, лихонько!

СТРЕЛЬЦЫ

Нету вам препонушки, а и нет запрету.
Гой, гуляйте,
Гуляйте весело!
Душите гой, и лих губите!
Смуту вражью...

ШАКЛОВИТЫЙ
(подойдя к будке)

Уходят... Слышь ты, строчило?..

ПОДЬЯЧИЙ
(тревожно)

Молчи уж... молчи!

ШАКЛОВИТЫЙ

Да слушай же!

Шакловитый обдумывает донос. Подьячий достает письмо а пробегает его, исправляя знаки и титлы.

ПОДЬЯЧИЙ
(прислушиваеться, успокаиваясь)

Слава тебе, господи! Промчало проклятых. Уж как я не люблю их, и сказать не можно. Не люди – звери, сущие звери! Что ни ступят – кровь, что не хватят – голову напрочь; а в домах плач и стоны. А все это, вишь, для порядка надо.

ШАКЛОВИТЫЙ

Слышишь ты! Живо в строку веди! "А мы живем ноне в похоронках; и когда господь утешит и все сохранится, и тогда объявимся".

ПОДЬЯЧИЙ
(пишет)

"В похоронках..." "Объявимся..." *(Шакловитому)* Готово!

ШАКЛОВИТЫЙ

Вручить царевне.

ПОДЬЯЧИЙ
(пишет)

"Вручить царевне."

ШАКЛОВИТЫЙ
(беря письмо)

Оборони тебя господь; смотри ж: помни.

ПОДЬЯЧИЙ

Да что ты стращаешь? Ей-богу, досадно! Невесть какая птица, туда ж кичиться хочет; полна мошна, так и пугать любо.

55

SHAKLOVITY

Silence! You should not meddle in things that don't concern you. What sort of man
I am you shall now discover. Messenger of evil, servant of the devil. Both now and
forevermore. Farewell!

He leaves.

SCRIBE

Go away, good riddance. Goodbye. There's a crazy fellow. He knows nothing of the
power that I have. Yet he seems to be a man of some importance, strutting around just
like a peacock. However, in spite of all his wealth and power my little baby calf is twice
as smart as he is. And I, lowly servant, I can still outwit him: I used the signature of
my dead cousin. 'Shame can do no harm to a dead man.' *(He picks up the purse.)* And
now the purse. *(opening it)* I'll wager it's a good one.

He counts the money.

MUSCOVITES
(offstage)

Master Koom and Mistress Kooma,
Mistress Kooma's Koom had a sister,
Sister's mister had a blister,
Sister's mister never kissed her.
Put Miss Kooma in bad humour,
To bad humour did he doom her.
Kooma's sister missed her Mister!

*The Muscovites enter and see the pillar. The scribe hides his purse. The scribe counts the money
by feel, under the counter, fearfully glancing at the Muscovites. The Muscovites examine the
pillar, walking around it and touching it in puzzled silence.*

Look brothers, look what has appeared right here in Moscow! Someone has been
busy putting up a pillar! Overnight a giant mushroom sprang up! Hold on, just a
moment, there's something very odd here. There is something written there. Written
there for all to see. I wish we could read it. No one can read it. Is there someone here
who's learned to read? No one. *(becoming thoughtful and looking at each other)* What a
bunch of fools we are, stupid peasants! Let's ask the scribe to read. Wait, you devils!
He's a civil servant. Works for the government. Well, what's wrong with that? Better
keep away from him. He can't frighten us. With proper respect, we'll ask him most
politely. We'll just address him with respect, according to the rules and regulations.
Careful brothers, let's not ask for trouble. *(to the scribe)* Could you help us, sir? What
is written here?

SCRIBE

What?

MUSCOVITES

Tell us what's written there?

SCRIBE

I'm just a stranger here, this is not my business.

MUSCOVITES

There's no need to be frightened, we're only peasants, poor and simple.

SCRIBE

Well, if you're poor simple peasants, then this busy clerk can't do your work.

MUSCOVITES

It's bribery! It's money, that's what he wants! Let him search our empty pockets.
He'll find a lot of nothing. Just the same he ought to tell us what is written on the
column. Grab him fellows, lift him. What for? Up high, there where the words are
posted. He cannot see the writing from the ground! Lift him brothers, so that he can
read the writing. That's right, old boy. Let's lift him with his hut together! We'll
make him read the sign to us. Come on fellows! Hi!

They lift the booth with the scribe in it and carry it towards the pillar.

SCRIBE
(Terrified, he leans out of the booth, waving his arms around.)
Hey there! Let go!

Ой-ли? Ой, не хоти узнать, с кем имеешь дело; ой, не нуди сказать, кто за человек я. Проклятый от века, дьявола ходатай, из нонешних будущий. Прощай.

Уходит.

ПОДЬЯЧИЙ

Скатертью дорога! Прощай. Вот чудак-то, право. Невдомек ему подьячая слава; и силен, кажись, и знатен, и богат, и нос свой вот ведь как воротит; да все ж, как посмотришь, хоть силен и знатен, а нашего ледащего телка глупее. А яз, червь презренный, похитрей маленько: под руку покойничка Ананьева подкинул: Мертвии бо срама не имут.*(Берет кошель со стойки)* Хе-хе. А ну, кошель, *(развязывает)* ступай ко на расправу.

считает деньги

МОСКОВСКИЕ ПРИШЛЫЕ ЛЮДИ
(за сценой)

Жила кума, слыла кума
а слыла кума недотрогой,
что слыла ль кума убогой.
Вот кум прознал, вот кум понял
как к куме бы подступить,
чем куме бы досадить.
И кум пошел, и кум нашел…

Пришлые люди выходят на сцену. Подьячий прячет кошель. Подьячий считает деньги ощупью, под стойкой, поглядывая, не без страха, на пришлых людей. Пришлые люди осматривают столб, обходят его, ощупывают, недоумевают молча.

-Что б на Москве такое приключилось? Вот-то, братцы, крепко столбушек сложили! Экой гриб повытянуло за ночь! Стойте, братцы, стойте; уж вот-то диво, право: столбушек-то с надписом, право слово, с надписом! Братцы, стойте, надпись! Тут-ко надпись есть! На столбе-то, братцы, надпись! Ай, прознать бы любо… Кто б казал нам, что тут? Что тут писано? Кто, робятушки, кто грамотный? Куси-ко локоть, парни! Мы не грамотны. Кто б читал нам, что тут писано? Да нету грамотных. Нету грамотных. Нету. Как же так? Вовсе нету.-*(Задумываются и переглядываются.)* Вот-то деревенщина: дура дурой! Подьячий-то на что? Стойте, черти! Он от властей поставлен. Он от властей, ребята. Что ж, что от властей? Ну, да как-то боязно. Что за боязно? А ну-ко, с почестью, да чинно подходи, ребята! А мы с почетом, да и с почестью, во всем, как по уставу надо. Не быть бы беде какой аль худу! Не быть бы худу! *(Подьячему.)* Добрый человек… Кажи нам, милый… Что тут написано?

ПОДЬЯЧИЙ

Ась?..

ПРИШЛЫЕ ЛЮДИ

-Что тут-ко писано?

ПОДЬЯЧИЙ

Избу строил с краю, ничего не знаю.

ПРИШЛЫЕ ЛЮДИ

-Да ты, друг, не сторожься. Ведь мы народ как есть убогой.

ПОДЬЯЧИЙ

Ась?.. Коли гол как сокол, так подьячего не для чего.

ПРИШЛЫЕ ЛЮДИ

-Ребята, взятку, взятку нудит. Ну, да с нас-то взятки гладки, не наживется, дьявол. Все ж, ребята, знать бы надо, что там на столбе за надпись. Вот что, братцы: вз車ем! Взымем! Кого? Подьячего да с будкой взымем, к столбу его: читай нам надпись! Ой, любо-то! Подьячего да с будкой взымем! Взымем, братцы, с будкой, да к столбу потянем! На тягостях на наших, да к столбу! А коли так: затянем про подьячего. Ой-ли, братцы! Ой!

Поднимают будку вместе с сидящим в ней подьячим и несут к столбу.

ПОДЬЯЧИЙ
(в ужасе высовывается из будки и махая руками)

Ахти!

MUSCOVITES

Once there was a fellow,
He had learned to read.
From his sins, this fellow
Never could be freed.

SCRIBE

Good people! Put me down, you'll kill me! Someone help me!

MUSCOVITES

Fellow built a cottage
On the edge of town.
Deep within that cottage
All his sins were found.

Peasants came to see him,
Simple and unread.
When they came to see him,
Bowing low they said -
(They set down the booth next to the pillar and bow to the scribe.)
'Gracious and noble sir,
Won't you show us pity?
Please won't you read to us
Since we are simple peasants.'
Then the scribe refused them.
He demanded money.
But the simple peasant
Does just what he pleases.
With great respect,
They tore his cottage to pieces.

They begin to dismantle the roof of the booth.

SCRIBE

Stop it! Let me down you bastards! Thieving pirates, idiots, let go of me! Have you had your satisfaction? I'll read it. Enough! Let me go!

MUSCOVITES

Let him read it! Why didn't you speak up? You thought you could get rid of us. We have treated you with exactly the respect you deserve, yet you try to extort money from your brothers.

SCRIBE

What? You're only trying to avoid paying your taxes. You'd rather live the high life, not caring about a thing.

MUSCOVITES

Enough! Read what's written!

The scribe looks at the inscription in terror.

SCRIBE
(to himself)

God! Protect me from the Streltsy!

MUSCOVITES

What's that? Why aren't you reading?

SCRIBE

What should I do?

MUSCOVITES

Read what's written!

SCRIBE

That's odd, there's something written here. *(to himself)* Oh God, the time of death is come!

He stares vacantly at the ground.

MUSCOVITES

Don't joke with us, brother! You won't fool us with your delaying. You won't get away with anything now that we're here! Read us what is written!

ПРИШЛЫЕ ЛЮДИ

-Жил да был подьячий
-Семьдесят годов.
-Нажил он, подьячий,
-Сотни две грехов.

ПОДЬЯЧИЙ

Ахти!.. Православные! Душат, режут, ахти!.. Помогите!

ПРИШЛЫЕ ЛЮДИ

-Ставил он избушку
С краю от села.
-Много в той избушке
Схоронил он зла.
-Сняли ту избушку,
Сняли, понесли.
-Кланялись подьячему
В пояс до земли.

(Ставят будку у столба и кланяются подьячему.)

Уж ты потешь нас,
Уж ты нас пожалуй:
Ты укажи нам, изволь,
Чего не знаем.
Отказал подьячий.
Взятки захотелось.
Тут робята принялись
За избушку,
Ой, почали таскать
Тесовую-то крышу.

Принимаются разбирать крышу на будке.

ПОДЬЯЧИЙ

Стойте, стойте, окаянные! Что вы это, сущие разбойники, что вы тут затеяли?.. Прочту вам... прочту... слышите!

ПРИШЛЫЕ ЛЮДИ

Брось, робята! Что ж ты ортачился, любезный? С чего теснить-то нас задумал? К тебе с почетом, а ты ровно что приказный,не по разуму. Как бы, мол, деньгу сорвать-то братии.

ПОДЬЯЧИЙ

Вот что! Вам бы только подати не платить, либо вам, гулливеньким, без заботы жить.

ПРИШЛЫЕ ЛЮДИ

Ну, ладно! Читай-ко надпись!

Подьячий всматривается в надписи, под влиянием неодолимого страха.

ПОДЬЯЧИЙ
(про себя)

Господи!.. от стрельцов лихих оборони!..

ПРИШЛЫЕ ЛЮДИ

-Что ж ты? Что ж не чтешь?

ПОДЬЯЧИЙ

Что мне делать?

ПРИШЛЫЕ ЛЮДИ

Читай нам надпись!

ПОДЬЯЧИЙ

Мудрено, нешто, писано. *(про себя)* Господи!.. пришла... пришла моя смертушка!..

Тупо смотрит в землю.

ПРИШЛЫЕ ЛЮДИ

Эй, брат, с нами не шути! На проволочках нас-то не подденешь. Тоже, ведь, прикинулся. Нет, шалишь, брат, нет, теперь попался. Читай нам надпись!

SCRIBE
(shaking)
My good Christians, I am putting myself at risk. You know too well how brutal the Streltsy are...

MUSCOVITES
Never mind, just read!

SCRIBE
(in despair)
The time has come to kiss my life goodbye! *(He reads the inscription.)* 'By the will of Heaven and to serve our great and noble Tsars, we, the regiment of soldiers assigned to Moscow, including gunners and infantry, in reprisal for injustice and treason, have discharged our duty.'

MUSCOVITES
The Streltsy wrote this. It must be the Streltsy.

SCRIBE
'Prince Telepnya was flogged and exiled. Prince Romanovksy was hanged for treason, acting as an informer. And the deacon Larinov, son of Vasily, has been beheaded.'

MUSCOVITES
Savage monsters!

SCRIBE
'For suspicion of conspiracy against the lives of our young monarchs...'

MUSCOVITES
Well, maybe they deserved it!

SCRIBE
'...And other Boyars beaten...'

MUSCOVITES
Which other ones?

SCRIBE
'...Brantsevy...'

MUSCOVITES
Who else was there?

SCRIBE
'...The Solntsevys.'

MUSCOVITES
What were they guilty of?

SCRIBE
'Embezzling currency and bread supplies... for hoarding food for themselves... forgetting God...'

MUSCOVITES
That's something else.

SCRIBE
'And then... whoever dares to slander the name of the detachments of the regiment based in Moscow...'

MUSCOVITES
(among themselves)
Listen brothers!

SCRIBE
'Or does not heed this proclamation, he shall be punished without mercy.'

MUSCOVITES
You're lying!

SCRIBE
(sincerely)
God is my witness, brothers!

ПОДЬЯЧИЙ
(вздрогнув)

Православные, страшны казни стрелецкие, неутомима ярость их лютая…

ПРИШЛЫЕ ЛЮДИ

Нам-то что? Читай!

ПОДЬЯЧИЙ
(с отчаяния)

Так пропадай моя головушка! *(Читает надписи.)* "Изволением божьим за нас, великих государей, надворные пехоты полков московских, и пушкари, и затинщики, от великих к ним налог и обид, и от неправды побили…"

ПРИШЛЫЕ ЛЮДИ

-Стрельцы, должно быть. Стрельцы ведь, значит.

ПОДЬЯЧИЙ

"…Князя Телепню кнутом да в ссылку; князя Ромодановского убили: туркам Чигирин сдал; тож убили думного дьяка Ларионова, сына Василья…"

ПРИШЛЫЕ ЛЮДИ

Вот-то звери!

ПОДЬЯЧИЙ

"…Ведал гадины отравные на государское здоровье…"

ПРИШЛЫЕ ЛЮДИ

Ну, это поделом.

ПОДЬЯЧИЙ

"…Еще бояр побили…"

ПРИШЛЫЕ ЛЮДИ

-Каких бояр?

ПОДЬЯЧИЙ

"…Брянцевых…"

ПРИШЛЫЕ ЛЮДИ

-Еще кого?

ПОДЬЯЧИЙ

"…Всех Солнцевых".

ПРИШЛЫЕ ЛЮДИ

-За что, про что? В чем провинились?

ПОДЬЯЧИЙ

"Чинили денежную и хлебную… передачу все в перевод… забыв страх божий…"

ПРИШЛЫЕ ЛЮДИ

-Вот оно что.

ПОДЬЯЧИЙ

"…А тем…кто словом злым реченных людей: надворную пехоту полков московскихъ обзовет…"

ПРИШЛЫЕ ЛЮДИ
(между собой)

Слушай, братцы!

ПОДЬЯЧИЙ

"…И тем… наш…милостивый указ… чинить без всякие пощады".

ПРИШЛЫЕ ЛЮДИ

-Врешь ты это!

ПОДЬЯЧИЙ
(искренно)

Как перед богом, братцы!

Входит в будку.

He enters the booth.

[5]   **MUSCOVITES**

God above! What grievous times are these! Our beloved homeland, so dear! Who can bring relief from bitter grief? You protect your children from distress. Yet there is none to shield you in return. Your oppression comes not afar, no remote and evil foe. *(Streltsy trumpets heralding the approach of Prince Ivan Khovansky are heard offstage.)* Your own children break a mother's heart. Your own blood is tearing the land apart. Through the raging turmoil of injustice, you've survived, survived this torment. You can bring relief from bitter grief. Who can ease our Mother's suffering?

They stand lost in thought.

BOYS
(offstage)

Hey there! Here they come!

WOMEN
(offstage)

They're coming, ladies! A song of welcome!

BOYS
(offstage)

Hey there!

MUSCOVITES
(listening)

Why the excitement? What's happening?

SCRIBE
(to the Muscovites, coming out of his booth)

The savage beast himself is here. Take my advice: disappear!

Exit scribe.

MUSCOVITES

Go on, to hell with you!

WOMEN

Sing to our White Swan these songs of welcome.
To our mighty Boyar sing glory!

BOYS

Here, clear the pathway!

STRELTSY

The Great One comes!

MUSCOVITES
(coming closer but looking offstage)

Just look at this! The crowd is huge! What's all the fuss about?

BOYS
(running onto the stage)

Make way, make way! The Great One comes! Stand back! He is here. Father of us all.

MUSCOVITES
(making way)

Brothers look, it's splendid!
Is this a holiday today?
Every day is a holiday.

STRELTSY
(entering)

The Great One comes! Make way, stand aside!

MUSCOVITES

The Streltsy are cut-throats one and all!

WOMEN AND BOYS

Make way for our Father!

STRELTSY

The Great One has come! Hail to you who trust in God! *(to the people)* Brothers of Russian blood! Prince Khovansky shall address you. So hear him with devotion. Our leader comes!

[6] *Enter Prince Ivan Khovansky. He carries himself easily with great arrogance. Behind*

ПРИШЛЫЕ ЛЮДИ

-Господи! Настало времечко! Ох ты, родная матушка Русь, нет тебе покоя, нет пути; грудью крепко стала ты за нас, да тебя ж, родимую, гнетут. Что гнетет тебя не ворог злой, злой, чужой, непрошенный, а гнетут тебя, родимую, все твои ж ребята удалые. *(За сценой стрелецкие трубы. Князь Иван Хованский творит обход.)* В неурядице да в правежах.Ты жила, жила-стонала, кто ж теперь тебя, родимую, кто утешит, успокоит?..

Стоят в раздумье.

МАЛЬЧИШКИ
(за сценой)

Ай-да! Весело.

ЖЕНЩИНЫ
(за сценой)

Ай знатно, бабы затянем песню!

МАЛЬЧИШКИ
(за сценой)

Любо!

ПРИШЛЫЕ ЛЮДИ
(прислушиваются)

Чтой-то, братцы? Чтоб это было?

ПОДЬЯЧИЙ
(пришлым людям, выйдя из будки)

Сам лютый зверь на вас идет, всяк человек пусть прочь дерет.

Уходит.

ПРИШЛЫЕ ЛЮДИ

Да ну те к дьяволу.

ЖЕНЩИНЫ

Белому лебедю путь просторен.
Знатного боярина славьте, славьте.

МАЛЬЧИШКИ

Эй, прочь с дороги! Слава Батьке!

СТРЕЛЬЦЫ

Большой идет!

ПРИШЛЫЕ ЛЮДИ
(надвигаются)

Толпа валит! Аль праздник, что-ль, какой?

МАЛЬЧИШКИ
(выбегают на сцену)

Дорогу всем. Большой идет; с дороги прочь, сам Батька пошел!

ПРИШЛЫЕ ЛЮДИ
(стороняться)

Чтой-то за праздник на Москве?
Вот так, братцы, любо, любо!
Что ни день, то пир горой!

СТРЕЛЬЦЫ
(выходят на сцену)

Сторонись народ, сторонись народ!

ПРИШЛЫЕ ЛЮДИ

Стрельцы-то, словно палачи!

ЖЕНЩИНЫ И МАЛЬЧИШКИ

Простор ему и слава!

СТРЕЛЬЦЫ

Сам Большой идет. *(к народу)* Люди православные! Люди российские! Сам Большой держит речь; внемлите благочинно, Большой идет!

Появляется князь Иван Хованский. Поступь плавная; держится высокомерно. За ним стрелецкие полковники и московские гости.

him come the Streltsy colonels and dignitaries of Moscow.

IVAN KHOVANSKY
(to the crowd)
Children, children of mine! Our Russian land (Praise God!) has plunged into darkness because of the vicious Boyars, their greed and vile corruption. Yes, my children.

He moves towards the crowd.

PEOPLE
Yes, yes, Great One! Truly, he is right!

IVAN KHOVANSKY
So, we've started to follow this noble mission. To save our young Tsars, we have resolved to crush this treachery. Are we right?

PEOPLE
Yes, yes! Glory to you! Glorious Father!

IVAN KHOVANSKY
(to the Streltsy)
You, Streltsy! Keep your muskets loaded! Praise God!

STRELTSY
We are ready, father!

IVAN KHOVANSKY
And now, in the name of the Tsars who rule us, we shall march through Moscow. *(to the crowd)* Sing for us!

PEOPLE
Glory come to you! Glory be to you!
Glory shall follow you through the noble deeds of yours!
Always the man of strength! As you defend us,
God's hand be with you!

Ivan Khovansky leaves, accompanied by Streltsy and people.

STRELTSY
The Great One Comes! Glory Father!

PEOPLE
Glory, Father, glory!

Prince Andrey Khovansky and Emma appear upstage, facing the audience. Khovansky is trying to embrace Emma.

[7] **EMMA**
Unhand me! Unhand me! I beg you, let go of me! I'm frightened!

[8] **ANDREY KHOVANSKY**
No, no! The turtle-dove cannot escape from the falcon!

EMMA
Mercy, mercy! I entreat you, mercy!

ANDREY KHOVANSKY
Hear her cry! Poor turtle-dove is caught in the claws of the falcon.

EMMA
(pulling away)
Listen to me! I know you well, you Prince Khovansky. You have murdered my father. You sent my betrothed into exile. You were merciless to my mother pleading for her life. And now what? Put an end to me, too. My fate lies in your hands.

ANDREY KHOVANSKY
You know, your anger makes you more lovely, just like a mother bird defending her little ones. Ah, only yield to me, my pretty one! Don't turn your glance away so modestly, you know you want me ...

EMMA
Let go of me! Or be done, and make an end of my life. So kill me!

ANDREY KHOVANSKY
Submit to me!

EMMA
God above! What is he saying now?

КНЯЗЬ ИВАН ХОВАНСКИЙ
(толпе)

Дети... дети мои! Москва и Русь (спаси бог) в погроме великом... от татей бояр крамольных, от злой лихой неправды. Так ли, дети?

Подходит несколько ближе к толпе.

НАРОД

Так, так, Большой! Правда, правда! Тяжко нам!

КНЯЗЬ ИВАН ХОВАНСКИЙ

Того ради подъяли мы труд великий, во здоровье царей благих крамолу извели(спаси бог!) Правы-ль мы?

НАРОД

Прав, прав! Болшому слава! Слава! Батьке, слава!

КНЯЗЬ ИВАН ХОВАНСКИЙ
(стрельцам)

Стрельцы, заряжены ль мушкеты? (спаси бог!)

СТРЕЛЬЦЫ

Все готово, Батька!

КНЯЗЬ ИВАН ХОВАНСКИЙ

Теперь в обход по Москве родимой, во славу государей! *(всем)* Славьте нас!

НАРОД

Слава лебедю, слава белому,
Слава боярину самому большому!
Лебедю ход легок,
Дай тебе боже здравье и славу!

Князь Иван Хованский уходит, сопровождаемый стрельцами и народом.

СТРЕЛЬЦЫ

Большой пошел! Слава Батьке!

НАРОД

Слава Батьке, слава!

Из глубины сцены, прямо против зрителя, появляются князь Андрей Хованский и Эмма; Хованский пытается обнять Эмму.

ЭММА

Пустите, пустите! Оставьте, пустите меня! Вы страшны!

КНЯЗЬ АНДРЕЙ ХОВАНСКИЙ

Нет, нет, нет, голубке не уйти от сокола хищного!

ЭММА

Сжальтесь, умоляю, сжальтесь.

КНЯЗЬ АНДРЕЙ ХОВАНСКИЙ

Ай, спесива стала голубка да в когтях у сокола.

ЭММА
(вырывается)

Слушайте! Я знаю вас: вы князь Хованский, вы убили отца моего, вы жениха изгнали, вы не сжалились даже над бедной матерью моей. Ну, что ж вы? Ну, казните меня, я ведь в ваших руках!

КНЯЗЬ АНДРЕЙ ХОВАНСКИЙ

Как хороша ты, пташка, во гневе. Словно за малых птенцов встрепенулася. Ах, полюби меня, красавица! Ах, не тупи ты очи ясные о сыру землю...

ЭММА

Пустите меня! Если надо - скорей убейте меня... убейте!

КНЯЗЬ АНДРЕЙ ХОВАНСКИЙ

Отдайся мне!

ЭММА

Боже мой, что он говорит?

КНЯЗЬ АНДРЕЙ ХОВАНСКИЙ

Не пытай меня! Поиму тебя в царицы, Эмма, и царским венцом украшу. Сними ты грусть-кручину с сердца сокола, голубка.

ANDREY KHOVANSKY

Do not torture me! I'll place you beside me on the throne. I'll make you Tsarina, Emma. Relieve the torment in the heart of the falcon, little dove.

EMMA

God above! What's this? Lord, you have always been my saviour!

ANDREY KHOVANSKY

Ah, don't be frightened, I shall watch over you. Submit to me.

MARFA
(by the pillar)

Submit to him. Give him your love!

ANDREY KHOVANSKY

Give your love. Emma!

EMMA

Prince, let go of me! Unhand me. Or I beg you to kill me now.

ANDREY KHOVANSKY

Then, by force, the turtle-dove will yield to the hungry falcon!

EMMA
(distraught)

Oh, save me! Oh, someone help me!

ANDREY KHOVANSKY

None can save the turtle-dove who's clasped in the claws of the falcon!

EMMA

Someone help me!

ANDREY KHOVANSKY

No, none can save you!

EMMA

Oh, save me!

ANDREY KHOVANSKY
(derisively)

No, no one's here!

MARFA
(coming between Khovansky and Emma)

I am.

ANDREY KHOVANSKY
(astounded)

Marfa!

[9] **MARFA**

Thus, O Prince, thou preservest thy constancy! Ah, my love, have I now become so hateful to thee? Didst thou not pledge thy faith and swear that thou never wouldst deceive me? Was it not in thy power to stay true forever to me, my love?

EMMA
(to Marfa)

Mercy, I beg you! I have done nothing wrong!

MARFA
(putting her hand on Emma's shoulder)

Another has replaced me. May you find happiness. *(to Emma)* My child, I shall protect and comfort thee.

ANDREY KHOVANSKY
(aside)

The devil himself sent this witch to me!

EMMA

How kind you are, I feel so safe with you.

MARFA

I know what happened here, I witnessed everything.

ANDREY KHOVANSKY

Like a snake, she spits!

EMMA

He is frightful! I can bear no more. He's relentless in his vile attack on me.

Боже, ты крепость и защита!

КНЯЗЬ АНДРЕЙ ХОВАНСКИЙ
Ах, не пугайся, ты ведь люба моя! Отдайся же мне!

МАРФА
(у столба)
Отдайся ему! Люби его!

КНЯЗЬ АНДРЕЙ ХОВАНСКИЙ
Люби меня! Эмма!

ЭММА
Князь, оставьте меня! Пустите. Я сказала, убейте меня... Убейте!

КНЯЗЬ АНДРЕЙ ХОВАНСКИЙ
Ну так силой сгибнет голубку сокол яростный!

ЭММА
(теряясь)
Спасите, спасите, о, помогите!

КНЯЗЬ АНДРЕЙ ХОВАНСКИЙ
Нет, нет спасенья голубке, что в когтях соколиных!

ЭММА
Помогите!

КНЯЗЬ АНДРЕЙ ХОВАНСКИЙ
Нет, нет спасенья!

ЭММА
Спасите!

КНЯЗЬ АНДРЕЙ ХОВАНСКИЙ
(дерзко)
Нет никого!

МАРФА
(разъединяя Хованского и Эмму)
Я здесь!

КНЯЗЬ АНДРЕЙ ХОВАНСКИЙ
(ошеломленный)
Марфа!

МАРФА
Так, так, княже, остался ты верен мне! Видно, скоро, мой любый, опостыла я; клялся, божился ты, мой княже, что не изменишь мне, только не в пору была та клятва, любый мой.

ЭММА
(Марфе)
Я не виновна! Пощадите меня!

МАРФА
(полагает руку на плечо Эммы)
Теперь другую имеешь: будешь с нею счастлив ты. *(Эмме)* Спокойся, ты со мной, дитя мое;

КНЯЗЬ АНДРЕЙ ХОВАНСКИЙ
(в сторону)
Сам бес толкнул сюда ведьму лютую.

ЭММА
Вы добрая, вы защитите меня.

МАРФА
Я знаю все; на грех мой, все я видела.

КНЯЗЬ АНДРЕЙ ХОВАНСКИЙ
Словно змей шипит!

ЭММА
Он страшен, я боюсь его. Он безжалостно преследует меня.

МАРФА
Зорким стражем о тебе я стану.Притуплю я когти злого сокола.*(лаская Эмму)*
Ты непорочна, чиста, невинна ты.

MARFA

Faithful protectress, I shall guard thy safety. I'll release the grip of the hungry falcon's claws. *(tenderly to Emma)* I know thy innocence, thy heart, thy chastity.

ANDREY KHOVANSKY

I will teach you to meddle in my affairs. You shall regret your high-flown foolishness. *(roughly pushing Marfa away)* And what has brought you here my pretty one? Recruiting? Looking for some converts?

MARFA

Is the time of repentance not upon thee? Thou must cease thy lies and vile seductions. Is a Boyar's vanity so powerful he is blind to a maiden's suffering?

ANDREY KHOVANSKY

Be quiet, witch!

MARFA
(bowing to Andrey)

Hast thou forgotten thy oath, Prince: not to enter into relations with the Lutheran faith, and to scorn the temptations of the Antichrist, or suffer eternal torment?

ANDREY KHOVANSKY
(frightened)

God! The Lutheran girl will denounce me! This can only lead to shame and degradation.

EMMA
(aside)

Now he is troubled and afraid, and with me he was so terrifying.

ANDREY KHOVANSKY
(aside)

No, I'll not play her games. I'll just dispose of her. *(to Marfa rudely).* My lovely, have you ever heard the tale about the fine young lad? He grew tired of his mistress, she had become so dull. *(Marfa watches Khovansky closely.)* So our fine young lad took care of her. And with no more delay, he whipped out his knife to kill her.

He throws himself at Marfa with a knife.

EMMA
(screaming)

Ah!

MARFA
(swiftly drawing a dagger from under her cloak and parrying his blow)

I heard the tale but with a different ending. But I am not prepared to bring about another's death. I'm not the one to whom thou makest final reckoning. *(excitedly)* My anguished heart has foreseen what thy fate will be: high in the mountains I see a cloister suffused with light.

EMMA

He is evil, he's a fiend! God protect her! Defend her with Thy holy power. For she has rescued me, yet I have no strength to rescue her.

ANDREY KHOVANSKY

She was sent by the devil himself just to torture me! Witchcraft protects her. My knife could not overcome her power. She's fearless, unstoppable and none can triumph against her will!

MARFA

And in the shining radiance. *(Trumpets are heard offstage.)* Souls of the dead are flying!...

PEOPLE
(offstage)

Glory be to you! O Great One, Glory!

STRELTSY
(offstage)

Glory to you!

EMMA
(to Marfa)

What's that?

КНЯЗЬ АНДРЕЙ ХОВАНСКИЙ

Уйму я тебя, досадную. Будет тебе бабе тешиться.(*нагло отталкивая Марфу*)
С чего ты право тут, красавица? Аль к бабе бабу тянет не в пору?

МАРФА

Не пора ли парню-то покаяться? Ведь не век же лгать на сердце девичье;
Аль в боярской спеси больше разума, чем в страданье девицы покинутой?

КНЯЗЬ АНДРЕЙ ХОВАНСКИЙ

Умолкни, ведьма!

МАРФА
(*наклонясь к Хованскому*)

Аль забыл ты присягу, князь:не вязаться с верой лютерской, презирать
прельщение антихристово, под страхом муки вечныя!

КНЯЗЬ АНДРЕЙ ХОВАНСКИЙ
(*испуганно*)

Господи! Донесет, поди лютая. На поруганье, на суд отцов сведет.

ЭММА
(*про себя*)

Он смущен, он боится? А с мною страшен был.

КНЯЗЬ АНДРЕЙ ХОВАНСКИЙ
(*про себя*)

Нет, не поддамся я, нет покончу разом с нею. (*Марфе дерзко*) Слыхала ль ты,
красавица, про некого молодчика: как с своей-то возлюбленной, что опостыла-
то, он, лих молодец, (*Марфа зорко следит за Хованским*) развелался без
околичностей. А и выхватил он острый нож…

> *Бросается с ножом на Марфу.*

ЭММА
(*вскрикивает*)

Ах!

МАРФА
(*выхватывает из-под ряски нож и отражает удар.*)

Слыхала, княже, и навыворот. Только не тот конец тебе я уготовила, и не от моей
руки сведешь ты счеты с жизнию (*Восторженно.*). Чут болящее сердце судьбы
глагол; видится в горних обитель дивно пресветлая…

ЭММА

Он ужасен, он злодей! Господи, спаси ее, щитом своим охрани. Она меня спасла;
бессильна я ее спасти.

КНЯЗЬ АНДРЕЙ ХОВАНСКИЙ

Дьявол сам нагнал злую ведьму пытать меня. Словно чурована, и острый нож
неймет ее! Бесстрашна, озлоблена и нет отныне запрета ей.

МАРФА

И в ней в луче чудесном. (*Вдали слышны трубы.*). Мчатся усопших души!..

НАРОД
(*за сценой*)

Слава лебедю! Большому слава!

СТРЕЛЬЦЫ

Большому слава!

ЭММА
(*Марфе*)

Что там?

МАРФА
(*прислушивается*)

Большой идет.

MARFA
(listening)

The Great One comes.

EMMA
(falling on her knees in fright)

God have mercy on me!

ANDREY KHOVANSKY

My father's here!

PEOPLE
(entering)

Glory come to you! Glory be to you!
Glory shall follow you through the noble deeds of yours.

STRELTSY
(entering)

Glory to you! Great One!
Glory be to you!

PEOPLE

We follow you, our Father!

STRELTSY

Glory to you! Great One!
Glory! God's hand be with you!

Prince Ivan Khovansky enters.

IVAN KHOVANSKY
(amazed)

What does this mean? *(Marfa bows to Ivan Khovansky)* Prince Andrey? *(to Marfa, as he passes her.)* Greetings Marfa! *(looking at Emma)* And not alone. A beauty, with handsome features, we find her pleasing. *(to the Streltsy)* You Streltsy, take her prisoner!

The Streltsy rush towards Emma but are stopped by Andrey Khovansky.

ANDREY KHOVANSKY
(standing in front of Emma)

No! Keep away from her, you demons; she shall not become your plaything. No, no, I order you to release her. If you dare oppose me you'll be sorry!

IVAN KHOVANSKY
(astonished)

God above! What's this! You dare? Hey you, you guards, take her!

ANDREY KHOVANSKY
(pushing back the guards)

Do not touch her!

STRELTSY

What shall we do then? Prince Andrey forbids us.

ANDREY KHOVANSKY
(to his father)

Prince, Father!

IVAN KHOVANSKY

Is this to be? Our commands are being disobeyed? Is this to be that our son ignores his father's orders?

ANDREY KHOVANSKY

Prince, my father!

IVAN KHOVANSKY

What? Who dares to oppose us? Who dares contradict our will? In the name of the Great Imperial Rulers of Russia the all-powerful...

ANDREY KHOVANSKY

Father!

IVAN KHOVANSKY
(pointing to Emma)

Hear our command and do not dare to disobey us. Seize and hold that girl and bring her to me for my amusement!

70

ЭММА
(в ужасе падает на колени)

Боже, ты крепость моя!

КНЯЗЬ АНДРЕЙ ХОВАНСКИЙ

Отец идет!

НАРОД
(выходя на сцену)

Слава лебедю, слава, лебедю!
Слава боярину самому большому!

СТРЕЛЬЦЫ
(выходя на сцену)

Слава лебедю, слава белому,
Слава, слава, Батьке честь!

НАРОД

Лебедю ход широк, дай боже !

СТРЕЛЬЦЫ

Слава лебедю, слава белому,
Слава, слава, Батьке честь!

КНЯЗЬ ИВАН ХОВАНСКИЙ

Батька идет. *(входит Князь Иван Хованский)* Спаси боже нашего Батьку.
Что такое? *(марфа кланяется Ивану Хованскому)* Князь Андрей!.. *(Марфе мимоходом)* Здравствуй, Марфа. *(рассматривает Эмму)* И не один, с красоткой... и белолицей... и нам приглядной...*(стрельцам)* Стрельцы! За караул ее!

Стрельцы бросаются на Эмму, но останавливаются перед Андреем Хованским.

КНЯЗЬ АНДРЕЙ ХОВАНСКИЙ
(заслоняя Эмму)

Нет, не отдам ее на пытку, вам, злодеям, на потехи! Нет, нет, не вам холопьям спорить с волею моей неукротимой.

КНЯЗЬ ИВАН ХОВАНСКИЙ
(в недоумении)

Что ж это?.. Спаси бог!.. Как так? А вы, стрельцы, взять ее!

КНЯЗЬ АНДРЕЙ ХОВАНСКИЙ
(отталкивая стрельцов)

Прочь, сказал я!

СТРЕЛЬЦЫ

Не можно, батька, князь Андрей мешает.

КНЯЗЬ АНДРЕЙ ХОВАНСКИЙ
(отцу)

Князь Батюшка!

КНЯЗЬ ИВАН ХОВАНСКИЙ

Будто и вправду мы более не главенствуем! Будтоб велели нам, что более не властны над сыном!

АНДРЕЙ ХОВАНСКИЙ

Князь Батюшка!

КНЯЗЬ ИВАН ХОВАНСКИЙ

Что? Кто может велеть нам? Кто смеет противиться нам? Во имя великих государей, преславных и всемощных...

КНЯЗЬ АНДРЕЙ ХОВАНСКИЙ

Батюшка!

КНЯЗЬ ИВАН ХОВАНСКИЙ
(указывая на Эмму)

Днесь вам, стрельцы, повелеваем неотложно: лютерку, что там,
отнять и к нам сюда доставить!

Стрельцы рьяно бросаются к Андрею Хованскому. Не замеченный никем, подходит Досифей; с ним несколько раскольников.

71

The Streltsy rush towards Andrey Khovansky. Dosifey enters, unobserved, accompanied by Old Believers.

ANDREY KHOVANSKY
(throwing himself at Emma with a knife)
Once I've killed her you can have her!

DOSIFEY
(restraining Andrey)
Stop! Heathen infidels! The devil dwells in you!

EMMA
(kneeling before Dosifey)
Ah, whoever you are...

IVAN KHOVANSKY
(angrily)
We are in charge here!

Dosifey holds back Khovansky with his hand and follows Emma.

EMMA
(to Dosifey)
Oh, save me! Don't let him murder me. Mercy!

DOSIFEY
Marfa, escort this girl back to her home, and be her shield and kind protectress. *(Marfa helps Emma to her feet.)* Give her comfort, my child!

MARFA
(bowing deeply)
Father, give me thy blessing.

DOSIFEY
[10]   *(blessing Marfa)*
Peace be with you. *(Marfa leads Emma away.)* And you, of the devil, again I ask: why do you rant and rage? The time is nigh when darkness invades our earthly spirits and destroys our souls! We have endured bitterness. Beaten down by life's travails, we withdraw our faith and piety from the church which alone can save us. Brethren, comrades, now is the time to fight for our religious belief! A noble battle, a fight for salvation. My spirit yearns, my heart freezes. Will you join our holy crusade? *(humbly kneeling)* Will you join the true believers?

IVAN KHOVANSKY
Streltsy! Quickly march! Go with the sentries and stay alert. Not one man shall pass through the gates to Moscow. May God preserve our city.

STRELTSY
Our Father's word shall guide us.

IVAN KHOVANSKY
The trumpet sounds. *(to his son, sternly)* Prince Andrey, resume your own command.

The people huddle together, perplexed. Ivan Khovansky leaves at the head of his Streltsy. Andrey Khovansky follows, his head bowed.

DOSIFEY
(with mystical emotion)
God above! Be our champion against the powers of evil.
Father! Be our guide through the powers of temptations.
Smile on us and keep Your children safe.
(The bell of Ivan the Great tolls. He bows deeply in the direction of the Kremlin and then rises quickly.)
Brethren, I'm troubled. Can we restore our faith? Sing brethren, sing the hymn of earthly renunciation. The time is near.

[11]   OLD BELIEVERS
Farther Almighty, save our souls from the path of heresy and sin.
(turning towards the Kremlin)
Give us strength to fight the power of the Antichrist.

DOSIFEY
(raising his arms)
Father, my heart is open to you.

72

КНЯЗЬ АНДРЕЙ ХОВАНСКИЙ
(занося над Эммой нож)
Так мертвую имайте!

ДОСИФЕЙ
(останавливая руку Андрея)
Стой! Бесноватые! Почто беснуетесь?

ЭММА
(опускается на колени перед Досифеем)
О, кто б ни были вы...

КНЯЗЬ ИВАН ХОВАНСКИЙ
(гневно)
Аль мы не властны?..

Досифей движением руку запрещает Хованскому и следит за Эммой.

ЭММА
(Досифею)
...Спасите, спасите! Не дайте сгибнуть мне! Сжальтесь!

ДОСИФЕЙ
Марфа! Сведи-ко лютерку домой. *(Марфа приподнимает Эмму.)* Да на пути защитой верной будь ей, чадо мое.

МАРФА
(делая поясной поклон)
Отче, благослови!..

ДОСИФЕЙ
(благословляя ее)
Мир ти! *(Марфа уводит Эмму.)* А вы, бесноватые, еще спрошу: почто беснуетесь? Приспело время мрака и гибели душевной, возможе Гордад! И от стремнин горьких, и от язвин своих изыдоша отступление от истиной церкви русской. Братья, други, время за веру стать православную. На прю грядем, на прю великую. И ноет грудь... и сердце зябнет... Отстоим ли веру святую? *(Смиренно кланяется.)* Помогите, православные!

КНЯЗЬ ИВАН ХОВАНСКИЙ
Стрельцы! Живо! В Кремль! Взять все караулы и зорким быть! Все входы и выходы стеречь неотступно. Господь хранит Москву!

СТРЕЛЬЦЫ
Костьми за веру ляжем!

КНЯЗЬ ИВАН ХОВАНСКИЙ
Труби поход! *(сыну строго)* Князь Андрей, в полковниках идти!

Народ толпится в недоумении. Князь Иван Хованский уходит со стрельцами, Андрей Хованский следует, понуря голову.

ДОСИФЕЙ
(в мистическом настроении)
Господи! Не даждь одолети силе вражьей.
Отче! Заступи от лихих твое откровение
на благо чадам твоим!..
(Колокол Ивана Великого. Досифей кланяется в землю к стороне Кремля, затем быстро поднимается.)
Братья! Тяжко мне! Возможем ли спасти? Пойте, братья, песнь отреченья от мира сего. Грядем на прю.

РАСКОЛЬНИКИ
Боже всесильный, отжени словеса лукавствия от нас!
(делают поварот к Кремлю.)
Силы соблазные антихриста ты побори!

ДОСИФЕЙ
(поднимая руки)
Отче! Сердце открыто тебе.

Уходит.

He leaves.

OLD BELIEVERS
(following him)
Lord our God! Bless us! *(offstage, barely audible)* Give us strength.

The curtain slowly falls.

Alexei Krivchenia as Ivan Khovansky in Vera Stroyeva's 1959 film of the opera

РАСКОЛЬНИКИ
(следуя за ним)
Боже наш Благий! (*Вдали, еле слышно.*) Подкрепи!

Занавес медленно опускается.

*Kira Leonova as Marfa and Anton Grigoriev as Andrey in Vera Stroyeva's 1959
film of the opera*

ACT TWO

At the residence of Prince Vasily Golitsyn. The furnishings are in a mixture of Moscow and European style. Prince Golitsyn is reading letters in his conservatory late in the evening. Candles are burning in a candelabra standing on the desk. The room looks out onto a small garden, surrounded by a beautiful lattice fence, mounted on stone pillars. It is dusk.

GOLITSYN

[12] *(reading)*

'Greetings, darling Vasenka, dearest light of my life. I cannot wait for the time when I finally see you again, my precious one. How sweet that day will be when once again I hold you in my arms, embracing you with all my heart! *(reading the letter)* As I was walking in the afternoon, reading a letter from the Boyars and one from you, I lost all trace of time, reading, thinking of you.' *(crumpling the letter in his hand)* The Tsarevna, despite her worries about the welfare of the two youthful Tsars, dreams day and night of our past love, inflaming herself with her memories of passionate encounters. *(standing up)* Dare I trust such declarations of love from a woman so ambitious? *(calmly)* Endless doubting plagues me, mistrust, suspicion... *(He becomes lost in thought, then continues decisively.)* No! I must not be fooled by meaningless, empty dreams which are clouded by my memories of pleasure. *(ironically)* Yes, I'll gladly trust you dear Tsarevna, yet with you one must proceed with caution. For you may change your affection, and then – off goes his head!... Best be careful, mighty Prince. *(picking up a letter from the desk)* Bah! A letter from my mother, the Princess. Messengers will hurry with royal treasures, to glorify the descendants of our great and honoured ancestors. *(opening the letter)* Much money is needed to accomplish these important deeds. *(reading)* 'You, light of my life, know how much I need you. You are more dear to me than my sinful soul. Keep pure in mind and body: you know this is what is pleasing to God...' *(dropping the letter)* What? Is this an omen? *(suddenly gripped by fearful superstition)* What fate threatens me? Dark thoughts torment me. We cannot comprehend these mysteries: my influence means little, my mind is useless. *(recalling the letter from his mother)* 'Remember to keep your body and soul chaste and pure, for God commands it...' *(He becomes lost in thought. Varsonofiev, Golitsyn's attendant enters.)* Who's there?

VARSONOFIEV

Noble Prince...

GOLITSYN

What?

VARSONOFIEV

A Lutheran minister has requested to see you.

GOLITSYN

Let him come in.

Exit Varsonofiev. Pastor enters.

PASTOR

I know your custom, Prince, of never turning away the requests of the sons of your beloved Europe. Forgive my boldness in interrupting your most elevated thoughts.

GOLITSYN

I beg you, Minister, to reveal your concerns to me. Do not be uneasy, tell me what is troubling you.

PASTOR

Anger and hatred, contempt, and a thirst for vengeance, a world filled with malevolent conflict, these things burden my heart.

GOLITSYN

What do you wish?

PASTOR

Young Prince Khovansky...

GOLITSYN
(anxiously)

Well?

PASTOR

...today, on the square...

76

ДЕЙСТВИЕ ВТОРОЕ

У князя Голицына. Обстановка в смешанном вкусе: московско-европейском. Князь Василий Голицын читает письма. Летний кабинет. Поздно вечером. На письменном столе князя зажжены канделябры. Перед зрителем, садик и красивая решетка на каменных столбах. Вечерняя заря.

КНЯЗЬ ГОЛИЦЫН
(читает)

"Свет мой, братец Васенька, здравствуй, батюшка мой! А мне не верится, радость моя, свет очей моих, чтобы свидеться. Велик бы день тот был, когда тебя, света моего, в объятиях увидела!" *(Всматривается в письмо.)* "Брела пеша… из Воздвиженска… только отписки от бояр и от тебя… Не помню, как взошла: чла идучи".*(сжимает в руке письмо)* Царевна, в заботах тягостных о благе государей младых, страсти кипучей предана, мечте о минувшем наслажденье всечасно предается…*(встает)* Верить ли клятве женщины властолюбивой и сильной?…*(спокойно)* Вечное сомненье во всем, всегда!…*(Задумывается; решительно)* Нет, не поддамся я обману мечты пустой одуряющих минувших наслаждений. *(не без насмешки)* Вам, конечно, верю я охотно, но с вами осторожность надобна, а то как раз в немилость, а там − голову напрочь!.. Осторожней, гетман-князь! *(у стола; выхватывает одно из писем)* Ба! Письмо от матушки княгини! Скачут послы с казною княженецкой для славы потомка великих, славных предков. *(развертывает письмо)* Для дел больших большие деньги надобны. *(читает)* "Ты, свет мой, сам ведаешь каков ты мне надобен, дороже душе моей грешной. Держися чистоты душевной и телесной; сам знаешь, как… то…богу любо…" *(роняет письмо)* Что это? Предзнаменованье, что ль?…*(под влиянием суеверного страха)* Чем грозит решение судьбы моей? Черные думы душу пытают; бесильны мы постигнуть тайну; ничтожна власть, ничтожен разум… *(вдумывается в письмо патери)* "Держися чистоты душевной и телесной. То богу любо." *(Задумывается. Входит Варсонофьев.)* Кто там?

ВАРСОНОФЬЕВ

Светлейший князь…

КНЯЗЬ ГОЛИЦЫН

Ну!

ВАРСОНОФЬЕВ

Лютерский священник что-то крепко пристал ко мне: видеть вас хочет.

КНЯЗЬ ГОЛИЦЫН

Так пусть войдет!

Варсонофьев уходит. Входит пастор.

ПАСТОР

Я знаю священный ваш обычай, князь, никогда не отвергать прошение сынов Европы, любимой вами; простите, я осмелился тревожить вас в высоких думах ваших!

КНЯЗЬ ГОЛИЦЫН

Прошу вас мне поведать, пастор, чем так смущены вы. Не стесняйтесь, прошу вас, скажите мне: что тревожит вас?

ПАСТОР

Злоба и ненависть, презренье и мщенья жажда, целый мирпроклятых противоречий терзают сердце мое.

КНЯЗЬ ГОЛИЦЫН

Что с вами?

ПАСТОР

Князь Хованский!

КНЯЗЬ ГОЛИЦЫН
(тревожно)

Ну!..

ПАСТОР

…Сегодня на площади…

GOLITSYN

Yes?

PASTOR

... offended a maiden...

GOLITSYN

Is that so?

PASTOR

... an unfortunate orphan...

GOLITSYN

Emma?

PASTOR

Yes, Prince.

GOLITSYN
(aside)

So that's what this is about. *(to the pastor)* You must understand, Minister. Be calm, I beg you. I cannot intervene in the affairs of the Khovanskys.

PASTOR
(aside)

My God!

GOLITSYN

But, if you have a request which falls within my powers to grant, something regarding possible benefits and privileges for you or your congregation...

PASTOR
(aside)

What an opportunity!

GOLITSYN

... I would happily consider your petition, as you know well where my sympathies. Speak, Minister.

PASTOR

I am uncertain... embarrassed...

GOLITSYN

Speak freely.

PASTOR
(aside)

He rejected Emma's cause: perhaps he will consider mine.

GOLITSYN

Well?

PASTOR

To keep the foundation of my beloved congregation's faith firmly implanted in their hearts, I entreat you, Prince, to allow us to erect a church in the German quarter – one more, only one. We know you are sympathetic to our cause.

GOLITSYN

I might suggest you dream less ambitiously, Minister.

PASTOR

Prince, I implore you. Hear me out.

GOLITSYN

Have you lost your senses, or has your ambition overcome you? You wish to fill all of Russia with churches! And, by the way, today I'm expecting the elder Khovansky here for a conference, as well as Dosifey. Would you say that it would be convenient for you to encounter them here?

PASTOR
(bowing)

My Prince, I understand. Forgive me...

GOLITSYN

Indeed? Farewell, Minister. Until we meet again, yes? Farewell. *(Exit Pastor. Golitsyn accompanies him and then returns.)* Impudent, sly rascal! A wolf in sheep's clothing... *(Varsonofiev enters.)* Again?

КНЯЗЬ ГОЛИЦЫН

Ну же!..

ПАСТОР

...Обидел девушку...

КНЯЗЬ ГОЛИЦЫН

Вот как!

ПАСТОР

...Несчастную сиротку...

КНЯЗЬ ГОЛИЦЫН

Эмму?

ПАСТОР

Да, князь!

КНЯЗЬ ГОЛИЦЫН
(про себя)

Так вот в чем дело! *(Пастору.)* Видите, гер пастор, о, прошу вас, успокойтесь; не могу входить я в дело частное Хованских.

ПАСТОР
(про себя)

Боже мой!

КНЯЗЬ ГОЛИЦЫН

Но если будет вам угодно просить, в пределах дарованной мне власти, об улучшеньях и о льготах возможных для вас, для паствы вашей...

ПАСТОР
(про себя)

Удобный случай!

КНЯЗЬ ГОЛИЦЫН

...Я с участьем приму прошенье ваше, ведомо уж вам мое расположенье. Говорите, гер пастор.

ПАСТОР

Я смущен... Я опасаюсь...

КНЯЗЬ ГОЛИЦЫН

Говорите!

ПАСТОР
(про себя)

Эмму отверг; быть может, пастор не отвергнут будет.

КНЯЗЬ ГОЛИЦЫН

Что ж вы?

ПАСТОР

Для соблюденья в сердцах любимой паствы моей основы веры живой я умолял бы, князь: дозвольте церковь возвести у нас, в немецкой слободе, еще одну, только одну, ведь к нам вы так расположены.

КНЯЗЬ ГОЛИЦЫН

Я предложил бы вам, пастор, поскромнее мечтать.

ПАСТОР

Князь, умоляю, выслушайте...

КНЯЗЬ ГОЛИЦЫН

Рехнулись что ли вы иль смелости набрались; Россию хотите кирками застроить! Да, кстати: сегодня я жду к себе на совещанье Хованского, senior, и что важно, Досифея; встреча с ними удобна ли вам будет, скажите?

ПАСТОР
(откланиваясь)

Князь, я понял. Простите...

КНЯЗЬ ГОЛИЦЫН

Да? Прощайте, гер пастор, до свиданья, не правда ль?.. До свиданья. *(Пастор уходит. Голицын провожает его и возвращается.)* Нахал, пройдоха... в овечьей шкуре волк!... *(Входит Варсонофьев.)* Опять?

VARSONOFIEV

Most noble Prince!

GOLITSYN

Well, what is it now, eh?

VARSONOFIEV

Excuse me, the fortune-teller you sent for this morning is here.

GOLITSYN

Have I employed a servant who has some intelligence, or an idiot?

VARSONOFIEV

Your pardon, Prince, a slip of the tongue. I meant to say the woman's here in search of your noble counsel.

GOLITSYN

That's better, send her in.

Varsonofiev exits. Marfa makes a quiet but formal entrance.

MARFA
(stopping)

Coming to see thee is like walking through the lion's den: your spies are lurking everywhere.

GOLITSYN

These are times of suspicion: times of deceit, greed and slander. *(with foreboding)* Our future lies enshrouded in mists of confusion, we squander our useless lives in fear and trembling.

[13]   MARFA

Wouldst thou not like to know about thy fate, Prince?
Shall I consult the spirit powers on thy behalf, Prince?

GOLITSYN

But how?

MARFA

Ask your servants for some water.
Golitsyn rings, Varsonofiev enters.

GOLITSYN

Some water to drink. *(At the table Varsonofiev pours water into a silver bowl and hands it to the Prince.)* Put it there!

Varsonofiev leaves. Marfa covers herself with a large black shawl and prepares to tell his fortune. The garden part of the stage is illuminated by moonlight. Marfa approaches the silver bowl of water on the table.

MARFA

Spirits of mystery, spirits of sorcery,
Souls of departed ones, free from earthly bonds,
I invoke you.
Spirits who drowned to death, spirits who froze to death,
You who must dwell in dark realms of eternity,
Hear me now.
Here stands a noble Prince seeking deliverance,
Burdened by doubt and fear, he seeks an answer here,
Reveal his fate.
(gazing into the water)
All is at peace in the heavenly sphere.
Bathed in the magic radiance of the light.
Powers of mystery ready themselves to speak.
Prince, they will now reveal the secret of thy destiny.
Thou art surrounded by guile and treachery,
Smiling faces encircle and smother thee.
Faces known and close to thee
Show thee a place stretching far into the distance,
Yes, I see it, truth has been spoken.

GOLITSYN
(alarmed)

What is the truth?

ВАРСОНОФЬЕВ

Светлейший князь…

КНЯЗЬ ГОЛИЦЫН

Ну кто там еще, а?

ВАРСОНОФЬЕВ

Колдовка, та, что намедни изволили вы звать, пришла.

КНЯЗЬ ГОЛИЦЫН

Своя ли голова на плечах у тебя, аль чужая?

ВАРСОНОФЬЕВ

Простите, князь, обмолвился. Та женщина, что часто к вам приходит за советом.

КНЯЗЬ ГОЛИЦЫН

Ну, то-то же. Позвать!

Васонофьев уходит. Тихо "обычаем" входит Марфа.

МАРФА
(останавливается)

К вам, княже, ровно бы в засаду попадаешь: холопы так и рыщут.

КНЯЗЬ ГОЛИЦЫН

Время потайных обманов, время измен и корысти. *(Суеверно.)* Грядущее сокрыто покровом туманным, трепещешь за каждый миг напрасной жизни.

МАРФА

Не погадать ли о судьбе твоей, княже?
Спросить велений тайных сил, владык земли, княже?

КНЯЗЬ ГОЛИЦЫН

На чем?

МАРФА

Вели принести водицы.
Князь Голицын звонит. Входит Варсонофьев.

КНЯЗЬ ГОЛИЦЫН

Воды… испить…*(Варсонофьев наливает воды в серебрянный ковш и подает.)* Поставь!

Варсонофьев уходит. Марфа накрывается большим черным платком и приготовляется к гаданию. Освещение садика и части сцены луною. Марфа подходит к столу, на котором стоит ковш с водой.

МАРФА

Силы потайные, силы великие,
Души, отбывшие в мир неведомый,
К вам взываю!
Души утопшие, души погибшие,
Тайны познавшие мира подводного,
Здесь ли вы?
Страхом томимому князю-боярину
Тайну судьбы его, в мраке сокрытую,
Откроете ль?
(Всматривается в воду.)
Тихо и чисто в поднебесьи,
Светом волшебным все озарено.
Силы потайные зов мой услышали.
Княже, судьбы твоей тайна открывается:
С коварной усмешкою лики злобные
Вкруг тебя, княже, плотно сомкнулися,
Лики, тебе знакомые,
Путь указуют куда-то далече…
Вижу светло, правда сказалась!

КНЯЗЬ ГОЛИЦЫН
(тревожно)

Что сказалось?

14

MARFA

Hear me! I see thee imprisoned in far-off lands brought down by bitter disgrace.
I see thee deprived of thy riches and power in exile, alone.
Thy fame cannot spare thee, nor wisdom nor valour, no efforts can change thy plight,
for fate has decreed it.
Thou shalt know bitter anguish of grief-laden hearts and privation, noble Prince.
The tears of thy suffering shall scald thy heart and teach the meaning of truth.

GOLITSYN

Go! (*Marfa slowly withdraws, looking around. Golitsyn rings. Varsonofiev enters.*) I don't
want her spreading her rumours. Go and drown her in the marshes! (*At these words,
Marfa rushes out. Varsonofiev pursues her.*)

(suddenly despairing)

So, that is what fate has in store for me.
And this is why my heart felt so troubled.
Disgrace and shame shall cause thy downfall,
and I shall soon die without friends or honour.
Once I thought I could trust in fortune,
my mission was to recreate our noble country.
I curbed the injustice of the Boyars,
I strengthened our relationship with Europe
and sowed the seeds of everlasting peace.
All the eyes of Europe were upon me
when I, as leader of our finest fighting men,
destroyed the army of the Polish barbarians;
or, at Andrusovo, when I attacked the vile invaders
who tried to capture our land from us,
our own Motherland, our native soul
still stained with blood of our Russian ancestors.
Now that is all forgotten!
Holy Russian land,
the wounds inflicted by the Tartars shall not heal.

Prince Ivan Khovansky enters.

15

IVAN KHOVANSKY

I entered without an announcement!

GOLITSYN

Then please sit down.

IVAN KHOVANSKY

Sit down, God above! There's the problem! We no longer know our places. You,
yourself, have abolished our ranks So we are equal to the serfs. Show me where my
place is.

GOLITSYN

Come now, Prince!

IVAN KHOVANSKY

Here, over there, or further by the doorway should I sit with servants or peasant folk?

GOLITSYN

Now this is something! That you, possessing influence and power, you, the head of
our invincible Streltsy, you're distressed about the Boyars' social standing.

IVAN KHOVANSKY

Listen! Do not mock, Golitsyn! You may boast of your petty little triumphs. But you
have compromised our honour, made us the laughing stock of clerics.

GOLITSYN

Of clerics?

IVAN KHOVANSKY

Enough, my Prince, you've had your entertainment.

GOLITSYN

At whose expense?

IVAN KHOVANSKY

You know the Tartars say all men are equal. But if you're not, well then, off with your
head. Perhaps you take your cue from the Tartars, Prince?

МАРФА

Княже, тебе угрожает опала и заточенье в дальнем краю.

Отнимется власть, и богатство, и знатность навек от тебя.

Ни слава в минувшем, ни доблесть, ни знанье - ничто не спасет тебя...

Судьба так решила.

Узнаешь великую страду-печаль и лишенья княже мой,

в той страде, в горючих слезах познаешь ты всю правду земли...

КНЯЗЬ ГОЛИЦЫН

Сгинь! (*Марфа медленно отступает, озираясь. Князь Голицын звонит. Входит Варсонофьев. Тихо Варсонофьеву)* Скорей утопить на "болоте", чтобы сплетни не вышло. (*Марфа, услышав последние слова Голицына, быстро уходит. Варсонофьев спешит за ней.*)

(*в порыве отчаяния*)

Вот в чем решенье судьбы моей,

Вот отчего так сердце сжималось:

Мне грозит позорная опала,

А там придет бесславье и погибель.

Так недавно, с верой крепкой в счастье,

Думал святой отчизны дело обновить я,

Покончил с боярскими "местами",

Сношения с Европою упрочил,

Надежный мир родной стране готовил...

На меня смотрели европейцы,

Когда, в главе полков, испытанных в боях,

Надменность сбил я заядлому шляхетству,

Иль под Андрусовым вырвал из пасти крулей жадных родные земли;

Те земли, кровью предков обагренные,

Принес я в дар моей святой отчизне.

Все прахом пошло, все забыто.

О святая Русь!

Не скоро ржавчину татарскую ты смоешь!

Входит князь Иван Хованский.

КНЯЗЬ ИВАН ХОВАНСКИЙ

А мы без докладу, князь; вот как.

КНЯЗЬ ГОЛИЦЫН

Прошу присесть.

КНЯЗЬ ИВАН ХОВАНСКИЙ

Присесть! Спаси бог! Вот задача! Мы теперь своих местов лишились. Ты же сам нас уладил, князь, с холопьем поровнял; где ж присесть прикажешь?

КНЯЗЬ ГОЛИЦЫН

Что ты, князь?

КНЯЗЬ ИВАН ХОВАНСКИЙ

Тут али ин где, подале на пороге, с челядью твоею, со смердами?..

КНЯЗЬ ГОЛИЦЫН

Не чудно ль это? Ты, доблестью и силою богатый, ты, властелин стрельцов неустрашимых, сокрушился о боярской причуды.

КНЯЗЬ ИВАН ХОВАНСКИЙ

Слышь, не труни, Голицын! Ты, кичась успехами своими, нас, и нашу честь, и сановитость предал дьякам на посмеянье.

КНЯЗЬ ГОЛИЦЫН

Дьякам?

КНЯЗЬ ИВАН ХОВАНСКИЙ

Ну, ладно ж, князь, натешился ты вдоволь.

КНЯЗЬ ГОЛИЦЫН

Над кем бы это?

КНЯЗЬ ИВАН ХОВАНСКИЙ

У татарвы ведь тоже все равны: чуть кто не так - сейчас башку долой. Уж не с татар ли ты пример берешь?

GOLITSYN

What? What was that? You're out of your mind! Control yourself, Khovansky!

IVAN KHOVANSKY

Ha, ha, that got you!

GOLITSYN

You dare to compare a Golitsyn with that accursed tribe... Then again, Prince, you know I am hot-headed and quick to anger. Perhaps that is what was decided at your Boyars' council meeting.

IVAN KHOVANSKY

May God be with you! I didn't decide: it was decided without me. But I shall find my rightful place as a Boyar and keep it, despite you.

GOLITSYN

Forgive my undue displays of temper, Prince Khovansky. I shall serve you as long as you would like.

IVAN KHOVANSKY

I venture to doubt that, Prince.

GOLITSYN

I beg your permission to continue what I was saying.

IVAN KHOVANSKY

Well, we deign to allow you, come what may.

GOLITSYN

Maybe it's true that my drastic measures angered the Boyars. I could not help it. But, strange as it may seem, believe me, I never once thought of you, Prince Khovansky. Although I knew very well that you envied that Boyar, you remember, in the reign of Alexey. He felt so offended by the seating, he crept underneath the table during the meal and sobbed and sighed to move a stone to pity, and whimpered just like a naughty little baby.

IVAN KHOVANSKY

What is this nonsense!

GOLITSYN

And then the Tsar took pity on his plight, so food and drink were brought to the Boyar...

And you, Prince Khovansky, you almighty commander who stormed through Moscow, reduced it to ashes, drenched the dust with blood - you are lost and cannot find your place.

IVAN KHOVANSKY

That's quite enough! I have listened to you most politely. I have not stopped this flood of sly malevolence. Now it is up to you to listen. Do not interrupt me. *(Golitsyn bows mockingly. Dosifey enters and stands looking fixedly at Khovansky.)* Do you know my ancestry? Royal blood is flowing in my veins. And that is why I won't abide your patronizing arrogance. What achievements? Be so kind, enlighten me: what are you so proud of? You mean that glorious campaign that you commanded when half your army died of hunger and not a shot was fired. What?

GOLITSYN
(heatedly)

You have not the right to judge my actions.

IVAN KHOVANSKY

And why not? Listen to him!

GOLITSYN

No! These things are far beyond your feeble power to understand!

IVAN KHOVANSKY
(angrily)

That's outrageous!

DOSIFEY

(He steps between the two Princes who stand motionless, not looking at each other.)
My Princes, calm your anger. This selfish pride is useless. Petty quarrels bring no relief for Russia. Princes, you set a fine example here. You've gathered here together eager to make a plan for Russia's future, you start to speak, then just like fighting cocks: peck, peck!

КГЯЗЬ ГОЛИЦЫН

Что? Что с тобой? С ума сошел... Опомнись, Хованский!

КНЯЗЬ ИВАН ХОВАНСКИЙ

Ага, забрало!

КНЯЗЬ ГОЛИЦЫН

Ты посмел Голицыну подставить племя проклятое... А впрочем, князь, вы знаете: горяч я, не в меру вспыльчив...ведь так решили в боярской вашей думе.

КНЯЗЬ ИВАН ХОВАНСКИЙ

Господь с тобой. Я не решал: без меня решили. Но место мое, боярское, я найду и соблюду наперекор тебе.

КНЯЗЬ ГОЛИЦЫН

Простите нечаянный порыв мой, князь Хованский. Я ваш доколе вам угодно будет.

КНЯЗЬ ИВАН ХОВАНСКИЙ

А позвольно усомниться, князь.

КНЯЗЬ ГОЛИЦЫН

Просил бы дозволенья докончить речь мою.

КНЯЗЬ ИВАН ХОВАНСКИЙ

Ну, соизволяем, куда нишло!

КНЯЗЬ ГОЛИЦЫН

Быть может, я бояр обидел мерой крутою, но неизбежной; только странно мне, что я, при этом о вас совсем забыл, князь Хованский, хотя и знал я, что вам завиден был боярин тот, что помните, при царе Алексие, за "место" обиделся гораздо и за трапезой, затискался под стол, горючими слезами обливаясь и хныча, точь-в-точь наказанный ребенок.

КНЯЗЬ ИВАН ХОВАНСКИЙ

Ну что ты брешешь там!

КНЯЗЬ ГОЛИЦЫН

Туда, под стол, тишайший царь велел боярину совать и мед и явства...
И ты, князь Хованский, ты, владыка всемощный, пред кем вся Москва лежала во прахе, кровью обливаясь, - ты нигде места не находишь!

КНЯЗЬ ИВАН ХОВАНСКИЙ

Довольно, князь! Я выслушивал тебя спокойно, я не припятствовал тебе в злоречье, выслушай и ты меня, и ты мне не припятствуй. (*Князь Голицын делает насмешливый поклон Хованскому. Входит Досифей и приостанавливается, не сводя глаз с Хованского.*) Знаешь ли ты, чья кровь во мне? Гедемина кровь во мне, вот что князь; и потому кичливости твоей не потерплю я. Чем кичишься? Нет, изволь, скажи мне: чем кичишься? Небось, не славным ратным ли походом, когда полков тьмы темь без боя ты голодом сморил?

КНЯЗЬ ГОЛИЦЫН

(*запальчиво*)

Что?.. Не тебе судить мои поступки!

КНЯЗЬ ИВАН ХОВАНСКИЙ

Вот те раз! что такое?

КНЯЗЬ ГОЛИЦЫН

Нет, не твоего ума это дело, слышишь ты!

КНЯЗЬ ИВАН ХОВАНСКИЙ

(*гневно*)

Что такое?

ДОСИФЕЙ

(*становясь между князьями. Князья стоят неподвижно, отвернувшись друг от друга.*)

Князья, смири ваш гнев, смири гордыню злую. Не в раздоре вашем Руси спасенье. Право, любо на вас глядеть, князья. Собрались для совету: так бы о Руси радеть хотелось? А чуть пришлись - ну ровно петухи: цап, цап!

GOLITSYN

Dosifey! Beware! You are too presumptuous. You forget the ways of Princes are not known to you, good fellow.

DOSIFEY
(calmly)

I have not forgotten. If I may, I shall remind you of my former station: for many years concealed and now forgotten.

GOLITSYN

What was concealed? What has been forgotten?

DOSIFEY
(grandly)

I, myself, because of my faith, renounced my princely station.

GOLITSYN
(to himself)

Prince Mishetsky?

IVAN KHOVANSKY
(to himself)

Mishetsky?

GOLITSYN
(confused)

It's true then... I heard rumours. But could not believe it. It cannot be that a Prince of Russian blood would spurn his noble ancestors and don the garb of clerics.

IVAN KHOVANSKY

That's correct! If you're born to princely station you should keep your princely station. Robes of the clergy are not for us. We don't wear them well.

DOSIFEY
(sternly)

O Princes, renounce these empty, vain illusions. Leave them. We've joined here in council: let's start, for time is passing.

GOLITSYN

Please be seated.

IVAN KHOVANSKY

If Mishetsky, who renounces his princely station, can be seated then I, too, ordained by God, may sit. We are seated.

DOSIFEY

Mishetsky is far from here, rest assured. I am not Mishetsky. I am the humble servant of God, Dosifey.

GOLITSYN

And praise be to God!

IVAN KHOVANSKY

Yes, it's true. Praise be to God!

DOSIFEY

Princes! Almighty God has surely sent his counsel and wisdom to you.

GOLITSYN

Let us begin. We must proceed straight to the heart of the matter that we are here to discuss.

DOSIFEY

Do you not truly realize, Princes, the cause of Russia's mortal danger and how we yet may save her? You are silent.

GOLITSYN

First we must understand where all our strengths lie.

DOSIFEY

Our strengths? In the love of God and holy faith.

GOLITSYN

Well yes, of course, that is understood. No, I mean other strengths!

DOSIFEY

What use to us are other strengths when true believers scatter through the country abandoning their homes?

КНЯЗЬ ГОЛИЦЫН
Досифей, прошу в пределах держаться. Ты забыл, что у князей обычай свой, не твой, любезный.

ДОСИФЕЙ
(спокойно)
Я не забыл, я напомнить только мог бы мое былое... Забытое, навек похороненное.

КНЯЗЬ ГОЛИЦЫН
Что забыл ты, что похоронил?

ДОСИФЕЙ
(величественно)
Мною самим отверженную мою княжую волю, князь.

КНЯЗЬ ГОЛИЦЫН
(про себя)
Князь Мышецкий?

КНЯЗЬ ИВАН ХОВАНСКИЙ
(про себя)
Мышецкий?

КНЯЗЬ ГОЛИЦЫН
(не без смущения)
Правда... Ходили слухи...Я... мне не верилось, чтобы теперь российские князья от предков чуралися и в рясы облекались.

КНЯЗЬ ИВАН ХОВАНСКИЙ
Правильно! Если ты родился князем, князем должен и остаться: ряса монаха для нас, князей, не по мерке шита.

ДОСИФЕЙ
(строго)
Да бросьте, князья, мечтания пустые. Ну их! Мы здесь собрались для совету: начнем, не терпит время.

КНЯЗЬ ГОЛИЦЫН
Прошу садиться.

КНЯЗЬ ИВАН ХОВАНСКИЙ
Если уж сам Мышецкий, открывший, садится так мне, Хованскому, и бог велел сидеть. Сели!

ДОСИФЕЙ
Мышецкий отсель далече. Спокойны будьте. Я не Мышецкий. Я божий раб, Досифей смиренный.

КНЯЗЬ ГОЛИЦЫН
И слава богу!

КНЯЗЬ ИВАН ХОВАНСКИЙ
Вестимо, слава богу!

ДОСИФЕЙ
Князья! Послал ли господь всемогучий совет и мудрость вам.

КНЯЗЬ ГОЛИЦЫН
Прежде всего, хотел бы я прямо к цели беседы нашей приступить.

ДОСИФЕЙ
Познали ль вы, князья, где святой Руси погибель и в чем Руси спасенье?.. Что ж примолкли?

КНЯЗЬ ГОЛИЦЫН
Да надо силы знать. Где эти силы?

ДОСИФЕЙ
Наши? В сердце божьем и в вере святой.

КНЯЗЬ ГОЛИЦЫН
Да, это-то конечно. Нет, иные силы?

ДОСИФЕЙ
Какие тут иные силы! Когда крестьянство домы побрасали и врозь бредут.

GOLITSYN

Well, that has ended this discussion!

DOSIFEY

And what do you think, Prince Khovansky?

IVAN KHOVANSKY

I? Just leave me my Streltsy, and I'll restore Moscow to order, and deal with the rest of Russia.

GOLITSYN

Just so. And with what form of government?

IVAN KHOVANSKY

What form? My own, of course.

GOLITSYN
(to Dosifey)

And what do you think of that?

DOSIFEY

Of government? If we abide by our beliefs and traditions, the people themselves will find our future.

GOLITSYN

Well, as for me, these old traditions bring no comfort.

IVAN KHOVANSKY
(to Dosifey)

Such an amazing mind he has!

DOSIFEY
(to Golitsyn)

Thy values have been tainted by thy foreign education. And so, with thee at their head, bring the Teuton rabble here to overwhelm us; and then, for all I care, dance and cavort with the devil, if it is thy pleasure.

GOLITSYN

Dosifey! How dare you call me traitor! I have not betrayed my birthright, unlike you. The love that I bear for Mother Russia carries more weight than your outmoded hypocrisy.

DOSIFEY

The rage thou witness in me is but a pale reflection of our people's rage! They hide in terror in the forests. They hate thy fiendish reforms.

IVAN KHOVANSKY

That's right! I agree. I myself am of your opinion. Many times have I tried to tell this haughty Prince. Many times have I explained: 'Prince, the old beliefs are right.' So what does he do? The Boyars' rights are kerbed as well.

DOSIFEY

Concern thyself with the Streltsy, Prince.

IVAN KHOVANSKY

So, what about them?

DOSIFEY

They serve Mammon, worship Belial, abandoning their wives and children. They prowl the land like savage creatures.

IVAN KHOVANSKY

So, what? I'm not to blame if sometimes they run wild from drinking. Were it not for the wine, they'd behave like perfect soldiers.

DOSIFEY

And thou stood back and watched? Thou idle, babbling good-for-nothing!

GOLITSYN
(heatedly)

What? What is this? In my own house, I'll not allow such lack of respect!

IVAN KHOVANSKY

He has insulted me unjustly!

GOLITSYN
(He stands at the table, turning his back on them.)

My friends, I must insist that we observe decorum.

КНЯЗЬ ГОЛИЦЫН

Ну, значит кончена беседа.

ДОСИФЕЙ

А ты что мнишь, Хованский князь?

КНЯЗЬ ИВАН ХОВАНСКИЙ

Я? Только оставьте мне стрельцов моих, и, видит бог, я Москву сберег и со всею Русью справлюсь.

КНЯЗЬ ГОЛИЦЫН

Так. А правление какое?

КНЯЗЬ ИВАН ХОВАНСКИЙ

Как какое? Мое, надеюсь.

КНЯЗЬ ГОЛИЦЫН
(Досифею)

А ты что мнишь об этом?

ДОСИФЕЙ

О правленьи? По старине мирской, по старым книгам, а дальше сам народ подскажет.

КНЯЗЬ ГОЛИЦЫН

Ну, к старине не слишком прилежу, признаться.

КНЯЗЬ ИВАН ХОВАНСКИЙ
(Досифею)

Вишь прыток; ась?

ДОСИФЕЙ
(Голицыну)

Не даром же в неметчине ты школу-то отведал! Ну что ж, веди на нас Теута с ополчением бесовским; Изволь, разводи у нас прохлады и танцы, дьяволу в угоду.

КНЯЗЬ ГОЛИЦЫН

Досифей! Изменой не кори меня; я от себя не отрекался как ты. К Отчизне любовь моя, быть может, выше твоих потачек старине мирской.

ДОСИФЕЙ

Во мне и в гневе моем народный гнев и вопль ты должен слышать, князь! Народ бежит в леса и дебри от ваших новшеств лукавых.

КНЯЗЬ ИВАН ХОВАНСКИЙ

Правда! Вот я:, я ведь тоже понял суть; князю-то кичливому все говорил, так же, все говорил: "Князь, не рушь ты старины". А он, глядишь, места боярам сократил.

ДОСИФЕЙ

Смотрел бы лучше за стрельцами, князь.

КНЯЗЬ ИВАН ХОВАНСКИЙ

А что стрельцы?

ДОСИФЕЙ

Мамоне служат. Белияла чтут, покинули и жен и домы, ревут и рыщут аки звери.

КНЯЗЬ ИВАН ХОВАНСКИЙ

Вона! Я ль виноват, зелена вина упились. Не будь вина, служили бы изрядно.

ДОСИФЕЙ

А ты чего смотрел? Эх, Тараруй ты, тараруй!

КНЯЗЬ ГОЛИЦЫН
(запальчиво)

Что? Что это? В моем дому прошу обычай соблюдать!

КНЯЗЬ ИВАН ХОВАНСКИЙ

Не обзывать меня напраслиной!

КНЯЗЬ ГОЛИЦЫН
(у стола, отвернувшись)

Гостей моих просил бы уважать, почтенный!

[16]   *From offstage comes the sound of the Old Believers singing. Dosifey, Golitsyn and Khovansky listen.*

IVAN KHOVANSKY

Is it not likely you are now resentful because I offered you my help, fighting men, advice and ample funds from my treasury?

OLD BELIEVERS
(offstage)

True believers, join as brothers, hear the holy call to battle.
We shall conquer non-believers!

DOSIFEY

I pray be silent! Show respect to these men of virtue who follow the path of God!

GOLITSYN
(alarmed)

What are you saying?

DOSIFEY

You, my lords, are only good at speech-making. *(Old Believers, carrying books on their heads, solemnly pass beyond the garden fence, accompanied by the crowd. Dosifey points to the procession.)* But there go men of action. See them, hear them: here they come!

OLD BELIEVERS

True believers, join as brothers, hear the holy call to battle.
We shall conquer sin and ungodliness, repel the powers of wickedness.
Over the forces of temptation, we shall triumph.

IVAN KHOVANSKY
(joyfully)

Good for you, my fellows, sing it!

GOLITSYN
(alarmed)

Who are these men?

DOSIFEY
(excitedly)

Shame and disgrace will fall on falsehood!
We will renounce all evil heresies!
We have cherished the garden of the Lord,
We believe in one true creed and doctrine!
We give glory to God above!

OLD BELIEVERS
(moving away)

Join as brothers!
Believers, we shall conquer...
Yes, we shall triumph!

GOLITSYN
(angrily)

Schismatics!

IVAN KHOVANSKY
(defiantly)

Splendid! Russia shall be restored through our faith and old traditions!

Marfa rushes in, out of breath.

MARFA
(to Prince Golitsyn)

Highness, Highness! I beg thee grant me life, not death, let me live!

GOLITSYN
(overcome with superstitious fear)

Sorceress! Sorceress!

IVAN KHOVANSKY
(rushing to Golitsyn)

God help you Prince, what is wrong? You're afraid of Marfa?

MARFA
(recognising Dosifey)

Father! Thou art here?

Вдали чуть слышно пение раскольников. Досифей, Голицын и Хованский прислушиваются.

КНЯЗЬ ИВАН ХОВАНСКИЙ
Или, быть может, я теперь осмеян за то, что помочь вам чинил войском, и советом, и казной своей немалой!

РАСКОЛЬНИКИ
(за сценой)
Победихом, победихом посрамихом, пререкохом,
Пререкохом нечестивых!

ДОСИФЕЙ
Пребудьте немы и внемлите доблим тем, в путь господа грядущим.

КНЯЗЬ ГОЛИЦЫН
(тревожно)
Что такое?

ДОСИФЕЙ
Вы, бояре, только на словах горазды, а вот кто делает. (*Раскольники, сопровождаемые толпой народа, торжественно проходят с книгами на головах за решеткой сада.*) Гляньте, гляньте: се грядут!

РАСКОЛЬНИКИ
Посрамихом, пререкохом и препрехом ересь, нечестия и зла стремнины вражие.
Перерекохом никоньянцев и препрехом!

КНЯЗЬ ИВАН ХОВАНСКИЙ
(весело)
Молодцы, ребята, лихо!

КНЯЗЬ ГОЛИЦЫН
(тревожно)
Кто молодцы?

ДОСИФЕЙ
(восторженно)
Пререкохом и препрехом
Никонианцев лжеучение,
Насадихом вертоград господень,
Соблюдохом веру правую,
Во славу зиждителя вселенные!

РАСКОЛЬНИКИ
(удаляясь)
Пререкохом...
Препрехом...Нечестивых...
Никонианцев.

КНЯЗЬ ГОЛИЦЫН
(гневно)
Раскол!

КНЯЗЬ ИВАН ХОВАНСКИЙ
(отважно)
Любо! Нами да стариной паки Русь возвеселится!

Вбегает Марфа, едва переводя дыхание.

МАРФА
(Голицыну)
Княже, княже! Не вели казнить, вели миловать!

КНЯЗЬ ГОЛИЦЫН
(с суеверным страхом)
Оборотень!.. Оборотень!..

КНЯЗЬ ИВАН ХОВАНСКИЙ
(бросаясь к Голицыну)
Господь с тобой! Что ты, князь? Это Марфа!

МАРФА
(узнав Досифея)
Отче, ты здесь?

DOSIFEY
(to Marfa)
What has happened to thee, dearest child of mine?

MARFA
Twilight was falling as I left the Prince. Out in the courtyard I felt a presence. One of the servants was lurking behind me. Soon it was clear, he was following me. There in the marshes, he seized me to choke me, *(to Golitsyn)* saying: those were thy orders, Prince. I tried to free myself from his attack, but he was possessed by spirits of evil. Vainly, I struggled, Death set his hand on me, I can no longer remember what happened, how I found the strength to escape from him. Praise be to God!... Tsar Peter's guards have come here... and they hold him in the courtyard...

IVAN KHOVANSKY, DOSIFEY, GOLITSYN
Tsar Peter's guards?

MARFA
Yes, a troop of guards was marching here, it seems.

Varsonofiev rushes in.

VARSONOFIEV
Shaklovity!

He runs off through the outer doors. Shaklovity enters through the side doors.

SHAKLOVITY
My Princes, the Tsarevna commands me to inform you. In Ismailov, a proclamation has been made: the Khovansky are guilty of high treason.

IVAN KHOVANSKY
The Khovansky!

DOSIFEY
(to Khovansky)
Forget thy scheming. *(to Shaklovity)* And what did Tsar Peter say?

SHAKLOVITY
That the Khovansky were at their games. It was time they were stopped.

Tsar Peter's trumpets are heard in the distance. Everyone looks astounded.

Yvonne Minton (Marfa) and Robert Tear (Golitsyn) at Covent Garden, 1982 (photo: Clive Barda)

92

ДОСИФЕЙ
(Марфе)

Что с тобой, дитя возлюбленное?

МАРФА

Шла я от князя по зорьке вечерней, только по задворкам, шасть - клеврет. Я домекнулась: следит за мной, видно. Было за Белгород близко "Болота". Тут при "Болоте" душить меня почал, *(Голицыну)* баял: "Ты наказал, княже". Я не поверила, я забранилась, а он, злодей, злобу выместить думал. Долго боролись, гибель грозила мне. Тут, уж не помню как, случай пришелся, только что силы, я вырвалась. Слава ти, боже!.. Петровцы подоспели... А на задворках и держут...

КНЯЗЬ ГОЛИЦЫН, КНЯЗЬ ИВАН ХОВАНСКИЙ И ДОСИФЕЙ

Петровцы?

МАРФА

Да, потешные прогулкой, что ли, шли...

Опрометью вбегает Варсонофьев.

ВАРСОНОФЬЕВ

Шакловитый!

Убегает на ружные двери. Входят боярин Шакловитый.

ШАКЛОВИТЫЙ

Князья! Царевна велела весть вам дать. В Измайловском селе донос прибит: Хованские на царство покусились.

КНЯЗЬ ИВАН ХОВАНСКИЙ

Хованские?

ДОСИФЕЙ
(Хованскому)

Мечтанья брось. *(Шакловитому)* А что сказал царь Петр?

ШАКЛОВИТЫЙ

Обозвал "хованщиной" и велел сыскать.

Все стоят в недоумении. Петровцы за сценой.

ACT THREE

The Streltsy quarter opposite Belgorod, on the Kremlin side of the Moscow River. In the distance is a solid wooden wall, made of enormous planks. Across the river, part of Belgorod is visible. It is noon. Old Believers pass through the quarter with a crowd of people.

OLD BELIEVERS
[16]   *(offstage, coming closer)*
True believers, join as brothers, hear the holy call to battle. We shall conquer sin and ungodliness, repel the powers of wickedness! *(entering)* Over the forces of temptation we shall triumph! We shall conquer, we shall shame them, we shall shame and conquer unbelievers! *(Marfa quietly appears out of the crowd.)* Death and shame to heresy. We shall conquer wickedness. We shall triumph! *(They disappear behind the wall.)* We shall conquer ungodliness! *(barely audible)* Come and join us. We shall triumph...

The stage gradually empties. Marfa approaches Andrey Khovansky's house and sits down outside it.

[17]   MARFA
Once a maiden went wandering
Through the meadows and marshes.
Through the meadows and marshes
She was searching for her lost lover.
Though her courage began to fail,
Sore and blistered her tiny feet,
Onward she wandered through the night,
But she could not find her lost lover.
To his own cottage she came at last,
Swift and silent she ran to the door,
Sharply tapped on the window pane
And she struck at the bell,
Hoping he would hear.
Do you remember, beloved one?
Ah, how you swore to be true to me!
Long have I languished through nights so dark,
And your vows were my consolation.
Like the eternal flame of God
We shall burn together.
We shall share in the brotherhood
Of the souls released by the cleansing fire.
You have broken the vows you made,
              (Susanna approaches unnoticed, and listens to Marfa's song.)
Mocked my love and devotion.
But, in death, you shall join with me,
With your loathed and despised Old Believer.

SUSANNA
(maliciously)
Sin! Sinner, repent thy ungodly ways.
Hell! Hell-fire will consume you! Devils sing in triumph!
Demons rejoice in thy downfall, and stoke the flames of perdition.

MARFA
Mother, have mercy, tell me what disturbs thee so.
Our days on earth are filled with suffering,
Hard our journey through the vale of tears.
(aside) Listen to me! I sound just like a prayer book.

SUSANNA
(listening)
Little maid, listen! Thou art cunning. Thou art a sinner indeed to sit alone here and to sing wicked songs to thyself.

MARFA
Thou crept up and thou spied on me. I was singing my song to myself. Thou hast stolen from me my grief; like a thief, thou hast stolen my secret woe. Mother, listen to me. I have never tried to keep my love a secret, and I shall not attempt to hide it

ДЕЙСТВИЕ ТРЕТЬЕ

Замоскворечье. Стрелецкая слобода против Белгорода, за кремлевской стороной реки Москвы. Вдали крепкая деревянная стена, сложенная из громадных брусьев. За рекой видна часть Белгорода. Время к полудню. Раскольники проходят по слободе в сопровождении толпы.

РАСКОЛЬНИКИ
(за сценой, приближаясь)

Посрамихом, посрамихом, пререкохом, пререкохом и препрехом, ересь нечестия и зла стремнины вражие. Пререкохом никоньянцев и препрехом! *(выходять на сцену)* Победихом, посрамихом, посрамихом, победихом ересь! *(Из толпы выделяется, незаметно Марфа)* Ересь нечестия, зла. Стремнины вражие и препрехом! *(Скрываются за стеной.)* Победихом... Нечестия... Презрехом... *(Едва слышно.)* И препрехом...

Сцена постепенно пустеет. К дому, занимаемому Андреем Хованским, подходит Марфа и садится на завалинке.

МАРФА

Исходила младешенька
Все луга и болота,
Все луга и болота,
А и все сенные покосы.
Истоптала, младешенька,
Исколола я ноженьки,
Все за милым рыскаючи,
Да и лих его не имаючи.
Уж как подкралась младшенька
ко тому ли я к терему,
Уж я стук под оконце,
Уж я бряк во звеняще колечко.
Вспомни, припомни, милой мой,
Ох, не забудь, как божился!
Много ж я ночек промаялась,
Все твоей ли божбой услаждаючись.
Словно свечи божие,
Мы с тобою затеплимся.
Окрест братья во пламени,
И в дыму, огне души носятся. *(Незаметно подходит Сусанна и прислушивается к песне.)* Разлюбил ты младешеньку,
Загубил ты на волюшке,
Так почуешь в неволе злой
Опостылую, злую раскольницу.

СУСАННА
(злобно)

Грех! Тяжкий, неискупимый грех!
Ад! Ад вижу палящий, бесов ликованье!
Адские жерла пылают, кипит смола краснопламенна!

МАРФА

Мати, помилуй, страх твой поведай мне.
Тяжка нам жизнь отныне стала
в сей юдоли плача и скорбей.
(в сторону) Кажись, по-книжному хватила!

СУСАННА
(прислушиваясь)

А, вот что! Ты лукавая, ты обидливая, а про себя поешь ты песни греховные.

МАРФА

Ты подслушала песнь мою, ты как тать подкралась ко мне, воровским обычаем ты из сердца исхитила скорбь мою! Мати болезная! Я не таила от людей любовь мою и от тебя не утаю я правду.

now from thee.

SUSANNA

God above!

MARFA
(approaching Susanna)
How he whispers words of love to me,
and his lips ignited mine with his kiss of flame.

SUSANNA
Back! Sacrilege! Speech of the devil. Words of impiety, thou triest in vain to ensnare
me.

[18] MARFA
No, mother. No, only listen to me.
Is it in thy power to comprehend the anguish burning in a lovesick heart?
Knowest thou not the joy desire can bring? Hast thou surrendered thy soul to thy
love?
Pardon, wouldst thou give, O mother, if thou knew the power of such love.
Pardon wouldst thou grant to such a soul who suffers love's relentless persecution.

SUSANNA
(filled with resentment and malice)
What do I hear? God above, what must I hear! Forces of evil try to tempt me, filling
my head with cunning speeches.

She goes towards Khovansky's house and sits in front of it.

MARFA
Do you remember, beloved one?
Ah, how you swore to be faithful!
Many dark nights have I pined for you,
and your vows were my one consolation.

[19] SUSANNA
God in Heaven above! Drive this demon far from my sight. Drive her away! My heart
is seized with hate, I must purge her of this profanity! *(to Marfa)*
Thou art deceiving me, thou art tempting me,
thou hast kindled in me flames of wickedness.
Sinner, thou shalt pay the price,
judgement shall fall on thee! *(Dosifey comes out of Khovansky's house.)*
I shall bear witness against thee. Tell of thy wicked ways! *(Marfa, seeing Dosifey, bows.)*
I shall prepare for thee fire to purge thy sins.

DOSIFEY
(stopping Susanna)
Why art thou raging so?

MARFA
(approaching Dosifey)
Father most holy, I have enraged our dear Mother Susanna by speaking the truth
without guile or deception.

DOSIFEY
Dear mother, what has happened? Remember that day long ago when Marfa rescued
thee from great misfortune? The torture chamber was ready for thee, for ranting and
raving, for vicious attacks, for madness.

SUSANNA
What's that to me? I shall not forgive.
(Marfa becomes lost in thought during the ensuing argument between Susanna and Dosifey.)
I have been deceived by her. And I have been tempted by her.
She has kindled in me flames of wickedness.
Sinner, she shall pay the price. Judgement shall fall on her!

DOSIFEY
Stop this spitefulness! Thy selfish, vain pride blinds thine eyes to others' pain.
(looking affectionately at Marfa) Profoundly hast thou pierced the heart of thine own
sister in suffering.

SUSANNA
I shall not relent!

СУСАННА
Господи!

МАРФА
(подойдя к Сусанне)
Страшно было, как шептал он мне,
а уста его горячие жгли пламенем.

СУСАННА
Чур…чур меня! Косным глаголом, речью бесовскою ты искушаешь меня!

МАРФА
Нет, мати, нет, только выслушай.
Если б ты когда понять могла зазнобу сердца исстрадавшего,
если б ты могла желанной быть, любви к милому отдаться душой,
много-много бы грехов простилося тебе, мати болезная,
многим бы сама простила ты, любви кручину сердцем понимаючи.

СУСАННА
(проникнута обидой и злобой)
Что со мною? Господи, что со мною. Аль я слаба на разум стала! Аль хитрый бес мне шепчет злое!..

Марфа идет к дому Хованского и садится на завалинке.

МАРФА
Вспомни, припомни, милый мой, ох,
не забудь, как божился,
много ж я ночек промаялась,
все твоей ли божбой услаждаючись.

СУСАННА
Боже, боже мой! Беса отжени от меня яростного. Сковала сердце мне жажда мести неугомонная.*(Марфе)*
Ты, ты искусила меня, ты обольстила меня,
ты вселила в меня адской злобы дух.
На суд, на братний суд,
на грозный церкви суд! *(Из дома, занятого Хованским, выходит Досифей)*
Про чары злые твои я на суде повем, *(Марфа, увидев Досифея, встает и склоняется перед ним.)*
я там воздвигну тебе костер пылающий!

ДОСИФЕЙ
(останавливая Сусанну)
Почто мятешися?

МАРФА
(подходит к Досифею)
Отче благий! Мати Сусанна гневом воспылала на речь мою без лести и обмана…

ДОСИФЕЙ
С чего бы это, мати? А помнишь ты, аль уж забыла, что Марфа от бед тебя великих спасла: в застенке дыбой пытали тебя, за злобу твою, за ярость твою, за блажь твою.

СУСАННА
А что мне в том! Не прощаю я!
(Марфа, в продолжение борьбы Досифея с Сусанной, погружена в тяжелое раздумье.)
Она искусила меня, она обольстила меня, Она вселила в меня адской злобы дух.
На суд ее, на братний суд, на грозный церкви суд!

ДОСИФЕЙ
Стой!.. Стой, яростная! Ты покусилась в злобе горделивой, *(с любовью указывая на Марфу)* на сердце болящее сестры твоей томящейся.

СУСАННА
Нет, не поддамся я!

DOSIFEY

Thou?... Thou Susanna? Servant of evil and handmaid of the devil, in thy raging madness, gates of hell are opened! I see around thee legions of demons, dancing and swirling, leaping and flying! *(Susanna covers her head with her hood and leaves slowly, pursued by Dosifey.)* Daughter of Satan, be gone! Thou offspring of Belial, be gone! *(He follows Susanna until she has gone. He then returns.)* So she's gone! She'll return no more. *(to Marfa)* Thou my beloved daughter, patience must thou have and thus shalt thou be faithful. So shall we save the holy name of Mother Russia.

MARFA

I suffer bitter torment. Grief and sorrow lie before me, desolate, abandoned, cast aside!

DOSIFEY

By Prince Andrey?

MARFA

Yes.

DOSIFEY

Has he harmed thee?

MARFA

He tried to kill me.

DOSIFEY

What wouldst thou do?

MARFA
(mystically)

Like two candles, lit for God,
We shall burn, yes burn, as one.
Our brethren share in cleansing fire,
And our souls with the flames fly to heaven above.

DOSIFEY

To burn! Terrible fate! Not time yet, not time yet, my daughter.

MARFA

Ah, father! Love is a torture far worse than death. Like a thief, it robs my soul of peace. For my God, I am unworthy and weak, and my love is an evil and wicked thing. Am I a sinner, Father? If so, I beg thee to end my life. Yes, kill me now. Don't delay, I beg thee kill me now and free my soul to find true salvation.

DOSIFEY

Marfa, my dear. My poor unfortunate child! Forgive me too, for I am first among sinners! The will of God must guide and lead us. Come, let us go. *(He leads Marfa away, calming her as they go.)* My child, be patient, and love as thou hast loved. And soon thy pain will be over.

Exeunt Marfa and Dosifey. Shaklovity enters from the opposite side.

[20]   **SHAKLOVITY**

The Streltsy nest is sunk in sleep. Sleep Russian people, your enemies are watching. Ah, I despair at your suffering Russia, my homeland! Who will appear, my country? Who will deliver you from sorrow? Or will your future be governed by the head of a ruthless foe? Does the evil German lie in wait to profit from your torment? Ah, motherland! Do not submit, no, no, do not bow your head before a foreign power. Sorrow tears at your children's hearts. O mother, remember us and care for us! *(pensively)* You suffered under the yoke of the Tartars, then you endured the oppression of the Boyars. To pacify the Princes, you let the Tartars govern you. To sweeten the Boyars, you raised them up to prominence. The Tartar rule has ceased to be. The Boyars wield their powers no more, but still you suffer, my country! God above, who from Thy highest heaven lookest down upon our sinful world. Thou who knowest the depth of the wretched grief that burdens our weary hearts, shine Thy light of holy wisdom on our motherland. Let Thy chosen one appear to restore our homeland to life and ease our pain. O God above, grant us Thy mercy and hear us: keep Russia free for evermore, dear God, from foreign might!

STRELTSY
[21]   *(offstage)*

Hey, you Streltsy, out of bed!
And shake the cobwebs from your head.

ДОСИФЕЙ

Ты?.. Ты, Сусанна?...Белиала и бесов угодница, яростью твоею ад создался! А за тобою бесов легионы мчатся, несутся, скачут и пляшут! (*Сусанна прикрывается капюшоном и сдержанно удаляется, преследуемая Досифеем.*) Дщерь Белиала, изыди! Исчадье адово, изыди!(*следит за Сусанной пока та не скрылась. Марфе*) Ну ее! Утекла, кажись. Вот то злючая! Ах ты, моя касатка, потерпи маленько и послужишь крепко всей древлей и святой Руси, ее же ищем.

МАРФА

Ох, нет, нет сердце, отче, видно чует горе лютое! Презрена, забыта, брошена!

ДОСИФЕЙ

Князь-Андреем-то?

МАРФА

Да.

ДОСИФЕЙ

Чинится?

МАРФА

Зарезать думал.

ДОСИФЕЙ

А ты что с ним?

МАРФА
(*в мистическом настроении*)

Словно свечи божие,
Мы с ним скоро затеплимся.
Окрест братья во пламеньи,
А в дыму и в огне мы с ним носимся!

ДОСИФЕЙ

Гореть... Страшное дело!.. Не время, не время, голубка.

МАРФА

Ах, отче! Страшная пытка - любовь моя. День и ночь душе покоя нет.
Мнится, господа завет не брегу, и греховна, преступна любовь моя,
Если преступна, отче, любовь моя, казни скорей, казни меня. Ах, не щади! Пусть умрет плоть моя, да смертью плоти дух мой спасется.

ДОСИФЕЙ

Марфа, дитя мое ты болезное! Меня прости! Из грешных первый аз есмь!
В господней воле неволя наша. Идем отселе. (*Уводит Марфу, на пути утешая ее.*) Терпи, голубушка, люби, как ты любила, и вся пройденная прейдет.

Оба уходят. С противоположной стороны появляется Шакловитый.

ШАКЛОВИТЫЙ

Спит стрелецкое гнездо. Спи, русский люд, ворог не дремлет! Ах ты в судьбине злосчастная, родная Русь! Кто ж, кто тебя, печальную, от беды лихой спасет? Аль недруг злой наложит руку на судьбу твою? Аль немчин злорадный от судьбы твоей поживы ждет? Ах, родная, а ни, ни, ой нет ты им лихим не поклонься, ворогам твоим! Вспомни, помяни ты детей твоих к тебе ведь ласковых и болезных. (*задумывается*) Стонала ты под яремом татарским, шла, брела за умом боярским; ты данью татарам вражду князей спокоила, ты "местом" боярским бояр служить понудила, пропала дань татарская, престала власть боярская, а ты, печальница, страждешь и терпишь! Господи, ты, с высот беспредельных наш грешный мир объемлющий, ты ведый вся тайная сердец болящих, измученных, ниспошли ты разума свет благодатный на Русь, даруй ей избранника, той бы спас, вознес злосчастную Русь-страдалицу. Ей, господи, вземляй грех мира, услышь меня: не дай Руси погибнуть от лихих наемников!

СТРЕЛЬЦЫ
(*вдали*)

-Поднимайся, молодцы!
-Аль на подъем вы тяжелы?
Поднимайтеся, стрельцы!

Hey, you Streltsy, out of bed!

(entering)

Are you ready for a fight?
Why can't you open up your eyes?
Did you drink too much last night?

SHAKLOVITY
(listening)

The beasts are stirring! *(ironically)* The docile, tender-hearted flock of Prince
Khovansky. Sing while you may, soon your songs will be over.

He disappears down the street.

STRELTSY

We'd feel much better if we had some liquor,
Where to find a drink is the problem!
We drank it all!

(They begin to sing.)

Ah, free from care our life would be,
If that liquor we drank last night
Wouldn't make us feel sick!
Was the liquor really bad? Or was it how much we had?
Hey, ho, never stop.
Hey, ho, drink until we drop!
Poor fellows, they passed out on their feet.
Don't disturb their slumber,
Gentlefolk, let the Streltsy get their sleep.
Hey, hey, filthy lout!
Hey, hey, kick him out!
Get up! Do your duty!
What a thing of beauty!
Ah, he's awake at last. Watch him stumbling around!
His poor head must be pounding
From the drink he had last night!
Streltsy lad,
We will smash and crash,
We'll defeat and beat.
We are mighty fighting soldiers.
Theft and treachery,
Lust and lechery,
We'll eliminate
Our villainous enemies!
As the Streltsy pass
Through the streets of Moscow
We will cut a path
Of complete destruction!
Hey, we'll survive!
Hey, look alive!
We're fearless,
We're bold and daring,
We shall safeguard
All of Russia,
We'll survive!
Hey, look alive!
Hey, hey!

The Streltsy women rush in and throw themselves at their husbands.

[22]   STRELTSY WOMEN
Oh, you disgusting stinking drunkards!
You good-for-nothing lazy bastards!
We'll sort you out!
You'll see just how! You have deserted wives and children.
You have abandoned your families.
Left them to perish from starvation!
Oh, you disgusting stinking drunkards!
You good-for-nothing lazy bastards!

-Собирайтеся, стрельцы!
-Али головушка болит?
Али сердце щемит?

ШАКЛОВИТЫЙ
(прислушиваясь)

Проснулось стадо! *(насмешливо)* Паства смиренная Хованских велемудрых! Не долог срок, песня скоро споется.

Шакловитый скрывается в улицу.

СТРЕЛЬЦЫ

-Опохмелиться было бы повадно.
-Аль за этим стало дело?
Вали валом!

(Запевают песню.)

-Ах, не было, ах, не было печали,
Только зла-презла настойка хмельная.
-Ах! Не вине-то быть виной,
А вина в вине запой.
Ой, ой, ой, ой, ой,
Ой, охти ж ли, ой, ой!
-Свалился, ах повалился стрелец.
Не буди его крещеный люд,
Дай отдохнуть стрельцу.
-Гой, гой, прибодрись,
Гой, гой, поднимись
С твоего ложа,
Ахти ж непригожа, ты стрелец.
-Гой! поднимался, ай, возбуждался стрелец,
Словно встать привелось
На грех со левой ноженьки, ой!
-А и рушь-порушь,
А и бей-разбей,
Волей-властью
Богатырской.
Всякой вред да зло:
Сплетню, воровство,
Что от ворогов твоих
Понаплыли-то!
Как пойшел стрелец,
Как пойшел родимый,
А по всей Москве
То погромом стало.
Ой, ах, стрелец!
Ах, молодец!
Не бойся
Ты не тревожься,
Стой на страже
Руси целой,
Гой, стрелец,
Гой, молодец!
Ой, ой!

Выбегают стрелецкие жены и набрасываются на мужей.

СТРЕЛЕЦКИЕ ЖЕНЫ

Ах, окоянные пропойцы,
ах, колобродники отпетые!
Нет казни вам, нет удержу!
Жен и семьи забыли,
деток малых покинули
на разоренье, на погибель.
Ах, окоянные пропойцы,
ах, колобродники отпетые!
Нет казни вам, нет удержу!

We'll sort you out! You'll see just how!
Unrepentant, cursed good-for-nothings!
Damn drunkards!

STRELTSY

See how our wives are always angry!
All that they do is nag their husbands.
Just to scold us and find fault with us!

(moving away from their wives)

Hey you women, be quiet!

A GROUP OF STRELTSY

Streltsy women, we're sick of your complaining!
Do your wifely duties, caring for you husbands!

A GROUP OF STRELTSY WOMEN
(peevishly)

Husbands, did you say, where are they?
They have not been seen for ages!

ANOTHER GROUP OF STRELTSY

You can never reason with a woman.
Men have greater wisdom, men are far more sensible.

ANOTHER GROUP OF STRELTSY WOMEN
(peevishly)

Where is all your manly wisdom?
At the bottom of a bottle!

STRELTSY

Woe is me! We used to be so happy,
Then our wives descended, now our fun is ended.

STRELTSY WOMEN

Woe on us, poor women, chained to drunken husbands!

A GROUP OF STRELTSY

Kuzka!

KUZKA

Eh? What?

STRELTSY

Please, good fellow, lend us your assistance.
Stop our wives from nagging us to death!

KUZKA

What's the problem?

STRELTSY

Help us!

KUZKA
(to the Streltsy women)

Ach, I don't feel so well,
Ah, see my hands are shaking.
These Streltsy wives are angry,
Their fury makes me frightened.
When they are raging, they are tyrants,
Overbearing, nagging shrews.
And hen-pecked Streltsy husbands
Dare not utter a single word.
Dear, gracious ladies,
Allow us a little song. All right?

STRELTSY WOMEN

All right!

STRELTSY

Bravo Kuzka!

KUZKA
(with a balalaika)

[23]
Gather round to hear the telling
Of a woman who was dwelling
In the alleys of our city.

Нет вам горя, окоянные,
Пропойцы! Пропойцы!

Будто бабы осерчали,
силы набрались, нам мешают!
Брань подняли, ополчаются!
(Отстраняясь от жен.)
Бабы, слышишь, довольно!

ГРУППА СТРЕЛЬЦОВ
Ой, да ахти ж, стрелецкие-то бабы,
Вот-то ополчились воевать с мужьями!

ГРУППА СТРЕЛЕЦКИХ ЖЕН
(сварливо)
Где мужья-то, где такие?
Были, были да сплыли!

ДРУГАЯ ГРУППА СТРЕЛЬЦОВ
Ох, трудненько бабам-то справляться
что с мужскою силой, а и мужней волей

ДРУГАЯ ГРУППА СТРЕЛЕЦКИХ ЖЕН
(сварливо)
Где ж бы тут мужская сила,
не в пропойстве ли та воля!

СТРЕЛЬЦЫ
Ай, ау! Нам не было ведь горя,
бабы налетели, горя захотели.

СТРЕЛЕЦКИЕ ЖЕНЫ
Горькое горе терпим мы и так уж!

ГРУППА СТРЕЛЬЦОВ
Кузька!

КУЗЬКА
Ась?...Ну?

СТРЕЛЬЦЫ
-Ты поволь нам, помощь дай, дружище!
-Слышь, утешь немилостивых баб-то!

КУЗЬКА
Что вы, други!

СТРЕЛЬЦЫ
Ну-кось!

КУЗЬКА
(стрелецким женам)
Ох, мне невмоготу, ох,
вот, вот совсем припешил;
строги да гневны, ой,
стрелецкие-то бабы;
гневны вовсе, не дозволят,
не дозволят, воспретят;
что воспретят-то бабы,
а велят совсем молчать.
Вы, бабы, госпожи,
позвольте, прикажи. Ау?

СТРЕЛЕЦКИЕ ЖЕНЫ
-Ау!

СТРЕЛЬЦЫ
Лихо, Кузька!

КУЗЬКА
(с балалайкой)
Заводилась в закоулках,
Где-то в темных переулках,
Заводилась баба злая,
Одинокая, большая.

She was neither young nor pretty.
All her energy was spent
On provoking discontent.
Causing trouble in the lives
Of adoring men and wives.

STRELTSY

How did she accomplish that?
Spreading harmful information
Was her only occupation.
She invented packs of lies,
To destroy and terrorize.
Her intentions were the worst,
May her evil name be cursed.
Gossip was her occupation,
Spreading harmful information.

STRELTSY WOMEN

Gossip slyly came a-creeping
As good folk at home lay sleeping
In the bedrooms of their houses
Devastating faithful spouses.
Honest people all beware,
Gossip travels everywhere.
Threatening both small and great
She does not discriminate.

STRELTSY

Boyars, princes, new reformers,
Gossip makes them all informers.
Gold and silver compensation guarantees co-operation.
Prison guards and civil servants
From this plague are not immune;
Lowly scribes who scratch and scribble
Dance to Gossip's tempting tune.

KUZKA

When her gossip is in season
People quickly lose their reason.
Lies and rumours fill your ear
Truth and honour disappear.
Once you've borrowed Gossip's throne
Then your life is not your own.
She will bring you degradation
Without a care for rank or station.

STRELTSY

We can think of nothing grander
Than to rid ourselves of slander.
Free ourselves from her attacking,
Send that gossipmonger packing!

STRELTSY WOMEN

Ah-u, Ah-u, Ah-u. Ah!
Join with us a take a stand.

STRELTSY

Join with us and take a stand,
Streltsy boys are in command!

STRELTSY MEN and WOMEN

Banish Gossip from the land.

KUZKA

Gossip, slanderers, be gone!

KUZKA, STRELTSY MEN and WOMEN

Be gone!

Стала думать да гадать:
Как бы людям помешать,
Как бы милым наплести,
Баб с мужьями развести.

СТРЕЛЬЦЫ

-Как же бабу ту назвать?
-Баба та сама назвалась.
Сплетней злою откликалась,
Много бед она творит,
На недоброе манит.
Ой, должно быть, проклята
Зла-презлая баба та,
Что сама пооткликалась,
Сплетней злою поназвалась.

СТРЕЛЕЦКИЕ ЖЕНЫ

-Сплетня и в семью прокралась,
Мигом по семье промчалась,
Сплетня семьи разорила,
А и деток-то сгубила.
-Бойтесь, бойтесь, молодцы,
Сплетни бабы злой-презлой,
Что грозит-то лих бедой,
Что казнит весь род людской.

СТРЕЛЬЦЫ

-Сплетня по застенкам шлялась,
Сплетня с палачом якшалась,
Всех доносчиков сманила,
Златом, серебром дарила.
-Не гнушалась и подьячих,
Тех, что перьями скрыпят…
Да гляди, поди, пускают
Жизнь людскую напрокат.

КУЗЬКА

Сплетня столько начудила,
Что и ум людской смутила,
Люди шепчутся и лгут,
Правды вовсе не берут;
Только сплетне поклонись-
От ума ты откажись,
Сплетня все вверх дном поставит
И прославленных бесславит.

СТРЕЛЬЦЫ

Как бы сплетню ту спровадить,
Больше б бабы не казалось,
От нее людей отвадить,
Сплетня ж ими бы гнушалась.

СТРЕЛЕЦКИЕ ЖЕНЫ

Ай, ау, ау, ау, ай!
Баба злая - сплетня та.

СТРЕЛЬЦЫ

Вы решайте, молодцы,
Посоветуйте, стрельцы…

СТРЕЛЬЦЫ И СТРЕЛЕЦКИЕ ЖЕНЫ

Чем ее нам извести?

КУЗЬКА

Сплетниц, сплетников…

КУЗЬКА, СТРЕЛЬЦЫ И СТРЕЛЕЦКИЕ ЖЕНЫ

На суд!
*Слышно, как где-то кричит с перепугу, как бы зовет на помощь, подьячий.
Затем он появляется, запыхавшись.*

ПОДЬЯЧИЙ

Беда, беда, ох, злейшая! Нет силушки! Ох, смертьюшка!

The scribe is heard, offstage, shouting for help. He enters, terrified and out of breath.

SCRIBE

Disaster! disaster! Ah, terrible! I can't go on, oh, death surrounds me!

STRELTSY

Crazy foolish idiot! Can't you take a little beating? More than likely you deserved it!
Listen to his weeping, what a coward! More than likely you deserved it!

STRELTSY WOMEN

See him tremble, barely breathing! He's quite delirious!

SCRIBE

It's worse than that. No, I haven't been beaten. No, no one threatened my life. No, no
one cursed my name, nor have I earned any insults!

STRELTSY

So, why are you running around like a madman. What makes you think you've got
the right to disturb us?

SCRIBE

Can't you see I'm frightened to death?

STRELTSY

Really! The poor old fellow, he must have forgotten the ways of the Streltsy soldiers.
All uninvited guests are thought of as the enemy, and do not leave our camp alive!

SCRIBE

My friends and brothers! Kill me, if it pleases you, that's all the same to me. But before
I die, let me tell you what I saw: the foreign troops are coming to destroy us!

STRELTSY

Foreign troops!

SCRIBE

Listen! I sat working hard in the Chinese quarter, I work so hard, I do my duty. I
wrote carefully striving for perfection, with heart and soul, for all God-fearing
people. When, suddenly... Horses galloping far off, the clash of weapons, voices
yelling. Armour clashing, screams of pain...

STRELTSY

It must be you they're after! What did you do to frighten them? You're the one they
want. They'll cut you in pieces. Truly, that's it!

SCRIBE

Swiftly they rode into Belgorod and headed for the Streltsy quarter. Then, this
heathen troop of devils attacked and surrounded your women and children!

STRELTSY

Liar! Lying fool!

STRELTSY WOMEN

God above, have pity on us!

SCRIBE

Suddenly, to the aid of the foreign troops, Tsar Peter's horsemen appeared from
nowhere, and all hell broke out. And then the Streltsy could do no more.

STRELTSY MEN and WOMEN

Woe, oh woe!

SCRIBE
(to himself)

So, now if I've sense, I'll get out while the going's good.

He slips out.

KUZKA

Streltsy! Let us ask Khovansky. He will know the truth, if these foreign horsemen
attacked our wives and children, and whether Tsar Peter helped them. Shall we?

STRELTSY WOMEN

Ask him!

STRELTSY

Ask him!

STRELTSY MEN and WOMEN

Father, father, hear our plea!
We implore you. Your children need you.

СТРЕЛЬЦЫ

-Что ты, дурень, брешешь? Видно, ловко трепанули! Поделом тебе, проклятый!
-Аль ты брешешь, дьявол? Вот так струсил! Поделом тебе, проклятый!

СТРЕЛЕЦКИЕ ЖЕНЫ

-Вишь дрожит-то, еле дышит! Словно в лихоманке!

ПОДЬЯЧИЙ

Ой, лихонько! Нет, не били меня, нет, не трепали меня, и ни уст моих,
ни слуха не оскверняли!

СТРЕЛЬЦЫ

Какая ж нелегкая сила шальная к нам, слышь, тебя невпопад подтолкнула?

ПОДЬЯЧИЙ

Страх попутал, смерть запугала!

СТРЕЛЬЦЫ

Вот что! Хитер ведь то же! Забыл аль не знал обычай наш стрелецкий, всякий,
незванный к нам ворогом зовется и жив отселе не уйдет!

ПОДЬЯЧИЙ

Отцы и братья! Мне теперь все равно, видно, уж смерть пришла, только не скрою
от вас я правды: рейтары близко! К вам мчаться, все рушат!

СТРЕЛЬЦЫ

-Рейтары!

ПОДЬЯЧИЙ

Слушайте! В Китай-городе был я на работе по долгу службы и честной клятве,
строчил грамоту, душу полагая за весь мир божий и за православных. Чу!..
Слышу: мерный дальний топот и коней ржанье, лязг оружья, латный стук и
дикий крик...

СТРЕЛЬЦЫ

-Видно тебя искали! Видно тебя ловить хотели! -Страха на них нагнал, поди!
-Слышь, напугал ты их! С боя взять тебя, с боя взять хотели! Чудно право!

ПОДЬЯЧИЙ

Близко уж было Белгорода, у самой слободы стрелецкой налетели злые вороги
на жен и детей ваших и окружили...

СТРЕЛЬЦЫ

Врешь, врешь, злодей! Неправда!

СТРЕЛЕЦКИЕ ЖЕНЫ

Господи, боже наш!

ПОДЬЯЧИЙ

Вдруг на подмогу рейтарам, откуда взялись, петровцы подоспели, и свалка
вчалась. Горе! Стрельцы изнемогли...

СТРЕЛЬЦЫ И СТРЕЛЕЦКИЕ ЖЕНЫ

Горе нам! Горе нам! Горе! Горе!

ПОДЬЯЧИЙ
(про себя)

Теперь наутек по добру да по здорову. Фить!

Исчезает тайком.

КУЗЬКА

Стрельцы! Спросим батю - правда ль то аль нет, что нам черт подьячий
понагородил о рейтарах да о петровцах. Так ли?

СТРЕЛЕЦКИЕ ЖЕНЫ

Спросим!

СТРЕЛЬЦЫ

Спросим!

СТРЕЛЬЦЫ И СТРЕЛЕЦКИЕ ЖЕНЫ

Батя, батя, выйди к нам!
Детки просят, тебя зовут.

*Князь Иван Хованский показывается под навесом терема и спускается к
теремному крыльцу.*

[15] *Ivan Khovansky appears at the top of the tower and then walks down to the bottom.*

IVAN KHOVANSKY
I greet you my children, I wish you all good fortune.

STRELTSY MEN and WOMEN
With joy and with glory we greet you, blessed leader!

IVAN KHOVANSKY
I come to answer your summons. Is some new misfortune threatening to harm us?

STRELTSY MEN and WOMEN
Tsar Peter's forces have come to kill us all!

STRELTSY
Lead us to battle!

IVAN KHOVANSKY
To battle? Do you recall how we waded through a stream of blood defending Moscow from her barbarous attackers? And we prevailed. Now things have changed, Tsar Peter is ruthless! Go home and wait my children, the hand of destiny will guide our future. Farewell, I leave you!

Exit.

STRELTSY MEN and WOMEN
God in Heaven, hear our prayer.
We beg Thee defend our homes and our children.
Father, grant us mercy, O Lord!

КНЯЗЬ ИВАН ХОВАНСКИЙ
Здорово, детки, на добрый час здорово!

СТРЕЛЬЦЫ И СТРЕЛЕЦКИЕ ЖЕНЫ
На радость и славу живи и здравствуй, Батя!

КНЯЗЬ ИВАН ХОВАНСКИЙ
Зачем меня вы звали? Аль беда какая с вами приключилась?

СТРЕЛЬЦЫ И СТРЕЛЕЦКИЕ ЖЕНЫ
Рейтары да петровцы губят нас.

СТРЕЛЬЦЫ
Веди нас в бой!

КНЯЗЬ ИВАН ХОВАНСКИЙ
В бой? Помните, детки, как мы по щиколку в крови Москву от ворогов лихих обороняли и соблюли? Нынче не то: страшен царь Петр! Идите в домы ваши, спокойно ждите судьбы решенье. Прощайте, прощайте...

Уходит.

СТРЕЛЬЦЫ И СТРЕЛЕЦКИЕ ЖЕНЫ
Господи! Не дай врагам в обиду
И охрани нас и домы наши милосердием твоим!

ACT FOUR

Scene One

A richly furnished banquet hall in Prince Ivan Khovansky's house. Prince Khovansky is dining; peasant girls are busy with needlework.

PEASANT GIRLS

Near the stream along the meadow
Sweetly slept a country lad.
He awoke to the song of a maiden,
He leapt from his bed of grass.
Though her song was but a dream
He rushed down towards the stream.
Bathed his face and hands so rough,
Then set off to find his love.

IVAN KHOVANSKY

Why must you sing such dirges? God save us! Where are your mourning veils? You sound as if you're at a funeral. Life's bad enough in our great Russia. There's no fun at all! We need no more reminders. But you persist in it. Your moaning, your weeping and wailing. It's lovely, cheers me up. I want to hear a song that sounds much livelier. Get on with it!

PEASANT GIRLS
(bowing to Ivan Khovansky)

We obey your command, noble prince.

IVAN KHOVANSKY

What do I command?

PEASANT GIRLS
(bowing even lower)

You command as you wish, noble Prince.

IVAN KHOVANSKY

Then sing me something better.

PEASANT GIRLS
(among themselves)

'Haidoochok'...'Haidoochok'?

They stop work.

IVAN KHOVANSKY

Why are you whispering? Sing it!

PEASANT GIRLS

All alone I sat awaiting,
As the candlelight was fading.
Haidook, Haidoochok,
As the candlelight was fading.
        (The peasant girls dance. Ivan Khovansky claps in time to the music.)
As the candlelight was fading
Casting shadows on the floor.

IVAN KHOVANSKY

All right! That's it!

PEASANT GIRLS

Casting shadows on the floor,
No one knocked upon my door.
Haidook, Haidoochok,
No one knocked upon my door.

One of Golitsyn's attendants enters.

IVAN KHOVANSKY

What do you want? How dare you come in here?

GOLITSYN'S ATTENDANT

Prince Golitsyn has sent me to warn you. Be on your guard, Prince!

IVAN KHOVANSKY

Be on my guard?

110

ДЕЙСТВИЕ ЧЕТВЕРТОЕ

Картина Первая

Богато обставленная трапезная палата в хоромах князя Ивана Хованскогоб в его имении. Князь Иван Хованский за обеденным столом. Крестьянки за рукоделием.

ДЕВУШКИ

Возле речки на лужочке
Ночевал я, молодец,
Услыхал я голос девичий,
Со кроватушки вставал.
Со кроватушки вставал,
Умываться бело стал,
Встал, умылся, собрался,
Ко девушке поднялся.

КНЯЗЬ ИВАН ХОВАНСКИЙ

С чего заголосили? Спаси бог! Словно мертвеца в жилище вечное проводят. И так уж на Руси великой не весело, не радостно живется, а тут бабий вой слышать забавно, и вопль, и скрежет: чудесно; Спаси бог! Веселую, да побойчей песню мне! Вы слышите?

ДЕВУШКИ
(делают поклон Ивану Хованскому)
Как поволишь, боярин-княже!

КНЯЗЬ ИВАН ХОВАНСКИЙ

Чего поволить?

ДЕВУШКИ
(кланяются глубже)
Как изволишь, боярин-княже!

КНЯЗЬ ИВАН ХОВАНСКИЙ
Чего вам там изволить?

ДЕВУШКИ
(между собой)
"Гайдучка"... "Гайдучка"?

Оставляют работу.

КНЯЗЬ ИВАН ХОВАНСКИЙ
Что вы шепчетесь? Пойте!

ДЕВУШКИ

Поздно вечером сидела,
Все лучинушка горела,
Гайдук, гайдучок,
Все лучинушка горела.
(Приплясывают. Князь Иван Хованский бьет в ладоши в ритм песенки.)
Все лучинушка горела
И огарочки прижгла...

КНЯЗЬ ИВАН ХОВАНСКИЙ
Бойчей! Вот так!

ДЕВУШКИ

Гайдук, гайдучок,
Все огарочки прижгла.
Гайдук, гайдучок,
Дружка милого ждала...

Входит клеврет Князя Голицына.

КНЯЗЬ ИВАН ХОВАНСКИЙ
Ты зачем? Осмелился войти?

КЛЕВРЕТ КНЯЗЯ ГОЛИЦЫНА
Князь Голицын велел тебе сказать: поберегись, княже!

КНЯЗЬ ИВАН ХОВАНСКИЙ
Поберегись?

GOLITSYN'S ATTENDANT

A grave and certain danger is threatening you.

IVAN KHOVANSKY

A danger? Are you completely crazy? *(to himself)* You dare disturb me here in my own home, issuing a warning - grave and certain danger. That's too funny, you make me laugh! Do you intend to frighten me? Lithuania rebels! Arise Khovansky! Prepare yourself! *(to his servants)* Hey, take this fool to the stables. The grooms can give him a good thrashing! Bring me wine! *(Golitsyn's attendant is taken away; to the peasant girls)* And you, can't you see I need amusement? Send in my Persian slaves!

[24] *Enter Ivan Khovansky's Persian slaves. They entertain him with dances. Shaklovity enters.*

IVAN KHOVANSKY

What do you want?

SHAKLOVITY

To see you, Prince.

IVAN KHOVANSKY

That much I can see. What for?

SHAKLOVITY

Without formality.

IVAN KHOVANSKY

And would you dare?

SHAKLOVITY

Prince!

IVAN KHOVANSKY

Well?

SHAKLOVITY

Our Great Tsarevna, disturbed by the suffering of our Russian people, has summoned you to join her in the High Council.

IVAN KHOVANSKY

Really! What's that to us? Let her summon all she likes. Have we not already offered our counsel to satisfy her wishes? And now, we think, there must be other advisors to serve her.

SHAKLOVITY

The first one she requested was you, Prince. For, without you, she said, the Council will have to be abandoned.

IVAN KHOVANSKY

So that's more like it! We shall attend with greatest pleasure. And once again our great Russian land shall have our wisdom at her service, God be praised! *(to the servants)* Hey, bring my finest robes of state. My prince's sceptre! *(to the peasant girls)* And you, sing our praises!

[25]   **PEASANT GIRLS**

The swan was swimming silently,
Ladu, ladu.
She swam to meet her beloved,
Ladu, ladu.
Her lover spied her swimming there,
Ladu, ladu.
He saw her there that snow-white swan,
Ladu, ladu.
                    (bowing to Khovansky)
He swifty swam to meet her there,
Ladu, ladu.
And now they swim together,
Ladu, ladu.
          (leading Khovansky by both hands towards the door)
Sing glory to the white swan,
Ladu, ladu.

As Ivan Khovansky reaches the threshold, he is suddenly stabbed. He dies with a terrible cry. The peasant girls disperse, screaming.

КЛЕВРЕТ КНЯЗЯ ГОЛИЦЫНА
Тебе грозит беда неминучая.

КНЯЗЬ ИВАН ХОВАНСКИЙ
Беда? Да не с ума ль ты спятил?..*(Про себя.)* В моем дому и в вотчине моейб мне грозит беда неминучая? Вот забавно, вот-то смешно! Пугать изволят князя!.. Литва проснулась! Вставай, Хованский!..Проснись и ты. *(слугам)* Эй! конюхам его! Пускай почествуют изрядно. Меду мне! *(Клеврета Князя Голицына уводят. Крестьянкам)* А вы, там на женской половине, персидок мне позвать!

Входят персидские рабыни Ивана Хованского и плясками развлекают князя. Затем появляется боярин Шакловитый.

КНЯЗЬ ИВАН ХОВАНСКИЙ
Ты зачем?

ШАКЛОВИТЫЙ
К тебе, князь.

КНЯЗЬ ИВАН ХОВАНСКИЙ
Знаю, что ко мне. Зачем?

ШАКЛОВИТЫЙ
И без обычая.

КНЯЗЬ ИВАН ХОВАНСКИЙ
И ты посмел?

ШАКЛОВИТЫЙ
Князь!

КНЯЗЬ ИВАН ХОВАНСКИЙ
Ну?

ШАКЛОВИТЫЙ
Царевна в скорби великой за Русь и за народ московский, зовет к себе, и ныне же совет великий.

КНЯЗЬ ИВАН ХОВАНСКИЙ
Вот как! Да нам-то что? Пускай себе зовет. Мы, кажись, немало и делом, и советом, и всячески царевне угождали. Теперь, небось, другие ей советчики послужат.

ШАКЛОВИТЫЙ
Тебя первым изволила назвать, князь; мол, без твоих услуг совет не может обойтиться.

КНЯЗЬ ИВАН ХОВАНСКИЙ
Вот это так. Теперь мы к ней охотно будем, и вновь Руси великой услугу нашим разумом окажем,.. спаси бог!... *(слугам)* Эй, лучшие одежды мне! Княжой мой посох! *(сенным девушкам.)* А вы величайте!

ДЕВУШКИ
Плывет, плывет, лебедушка,
Ладу-ладу,
Плывет навстречу лебедю,
Ладу-ладу.
Сустрел, сустрел лебедушку,
Ладу-ладу,
Сустрел тот лебедь белый,
Ладу-ладу.
(кланяются Хованскому)
Пошел ходить с лебедушкой,
Ладу-ладу,
С подруженькой помолвился,
Ладу-ладу,
(Князь Иван Хованский, поддерживаемый под руки холопами, направляется к дверям.)
И пели славу лебедю,
Ладу-ладу,

Князя Хованского внезапно убивают в дверях. Он падает мертвым со страшным криком. Девушки разбегаются с визгом.

SHAKLOVITY
(going up to Khovansky's body)

Sing glory to the white swan,
Ladu, ladu.

He laughs. The curtain falls.

[14] # Scene Two

Moscow. The square before the church of St Basil. As the curtain rises, Muscovites are examining the outside of the church. A detachment of soldiers, armed with sabres and lances enter and line the road to the church. Muscovites hurriedly gather opposite them. Horsemen appear. Behind them is a dilapidated carriage escorted by soldiers. The people watch the procession with curiosity.

PEOPLE

See him! Look there!
They're sending him to exile! He'll not be back. *(The procession disappears slowly. The soldiers follow.)* May God forgive your sins. Pray to God to grant your soul divine salvation!

The people slowly follow the procession, their heads uncovered. Dosifey enters.

DOSIFEY
(watching the procession move off)

So destiny's decree has been fulfilled. No man can change the decision or the will of God. Prince Golitsyn, our almighty Golitsyn, Russia's pride and glory, disgraced and exiled. And now the sole remaining traces of his life are carriage tracks receding in the distance. We never shall forget Khovansky, the Streltsy's great commander. Through stupid arrogance and pride, he brought about his own destruction. Let us not forget his son, the Prince. His future will not be the throne of holy Russia...

Marfa enters.

MARFA

Father!

DOSIFEY

Yes? Hast thou learned something new, my daughter. Has the Great Assembly passed a judgement against us? We who would serve our ancient Russia?

MARFA

O father, mortal peril approaches. Soon Tsar Peter's horsemen will surround our holy shrine. Then, without mercy, they will attack and destroy us.

DOSIFEY

You're sure of that?

MARFA

Yes!

DOSIFEY

It's final? So, now the time has come to win, through martyrdom, the crown of life everlasting! Marfa! Keep Prince Andrey near thee, for he may weaken and his soul might not be saved.

MARFA

I will.

DOSIFEY

Be strong, my little dove, and trust the power of love. And glory everlasting will crown thy name. Farewell!

Exit.

MARFA
(excitedly)

So now the time has come to unite before our Lord,
In fire and flames together we find life eternal.

Andrey Khovansky enters in a state of great agitation.

114

(подойдя к трупу Хованского)

Белому лебедю, слава
Ладу-ладу.

Хохочет. Занавес падает.

Картина вторая

Москва. Площадь перед церковью Василия Блаженного. Московский люд толпится, рассматривая наружный вид церкви. Входит партия рейтар, вооруженных мечами. Рейтары становятся шпалерами, спиной к церкви. Народ поспешно группируется в противоположную от них сторону. Показываются рейтары на конях, за ними колымага, сопровождаемая также рейтарами. Народ с любопытством всматривается в поезд.

МОСКОВСКИЙ ЛЮД
-Глянь-ко: везут.
-Везут, везут взаправду.
(Поезд медленно удаляется. Рейтары, стоявшие шпалерами, следуют за ним.) Прости тебе господь! Помоги тебе господь в твоей неволе!

Народ медленно следует с открытыми головами вслед за поездом. На площади появляется Досифей.

ДОСИФЕЙ
(вслед удаляющемуся поезду)
Свершилося решение судьбы неумолимой и грозной, как сам страшный судия! Князь Голицын, властелин всевластный, князь Голицын, гордость Руси целой, - опальный выслан вдаль, а здесь от поезда печального его одни лишь колеи остались. А видно мудрым был начальник Стрелецкого приказа! Из-за кичливости своей себя и ближних погубил, и княжичу, поди не сдобровать: царем, вишь, его на Москве предназначали...

Входит Марфа.
МАРФА
Отче!

ДОСИФЕЙ
А?.. Что ж, прознала ты, голубка, чем решил Совет великий против нас в попрек древлей Руси, ее же ищем?

МАРФА
Не скрою, отче, горе грозит нам! Велено рейтарам окружить нас в святом скиту и без пощады, без сожаленья губить нас.
ДОСИФЕЙ
Вот что.

МАРФА
Да!

ДОСИФЕЙ
Так вот что? Теперь приспело время в огне и пламени принять венец славы вечные! Марфа, возьми с собой Андрея-князя, не то ослабнет и не подвигнется.
МАРФА
Возьму.

ДОСИФЕЙ
Терпи, голубушка, люби, как ты любила, и славы венцом покроется имя твое. Прости!
Уходит.
МАРФА
(восторженно)
Теперь приспело время принять от господа
в огне и пламени венец славы вечныя!

Андрей Хованский поспешно входит, в сильном волнении.

ANDREY KHOVANSKY
(to Marfa)

Here you are, you serpent! *(angrily grabbing Marfa's hand)* Ah, you witch! Where is my Emma? Where have you concealed her? I want my Emma, return my own beloved! Where is she? I want her now. Give her back!

MARFA

Emma has been taken by the foreign soldiers. May God be with her! Soon she will join her betrothed, far away, who thou did banish from here. Together they may prosper.

ANDREY KHOVANSKY

Her betrothed! Lying snake! I don't believe you! I shall assemble all my Streltsy. All of Moscow will denounce your name. For treason you will die.

MARFA

I'll die? Clearly thou hast not realised, Prince,
that thy fate has already been determined.
Destiny commands and thou must surely follow.
Fate will never lie or deceive.
Thy course is steered by an unrelenting...

ANDREY KHOVANSKY

Emma, Emma return to me!

MARFA

Thy proud father hast been killed through vilest treachery.
His sinful body lies forgotten and unburied.
Only the bitter wind to consecrate his body.
Only the birds of prey to satisfy their hunger.
And thou art the next, for they seek thee throughout Moscow.

ANDREY KHOVANSKY

You are lying to me. May you be damned to hell! You have consorted to evil powers of darkness and together you cast a wicked spell. You have bewitched my heart and destroyed me! As a sorceress, shall I denounce you and the Streltsy will accuse you of black magic. You will burn at the stake before the people.

MARFA

So, call the Streltsy!

ANDREY KHOVANSKY
(haughtily)

The Streltsy?

MARFA

Call them!

Andrey blows his horn. A bell tolls.

ANDREY KHOVANSKY

What was that?

MARFA

Call them again!

Andrey Khovansky blows his horn again. As the great bell of the cathedral tolls, the Streltsy, followed by their women, enter, carrying execution blocks and halberds.

ANDREY KHOVANSKY

Father in Heaven! All is over. Marfa, I beg you. Protect me now!

MARFA
(hurriedly leading Khovansky away)

Can they not hear thy call? So be it Prince, I shall conceal thee in a place of refuge. Stay close to me. Be brave my Prince and follow me!

The Streltsy set up execution blocks and lay their halberds on them with the blades upwards.

STRELTSY WOMEN

Show them no mercy. Make these bastards suffer! May they all burn in hell, burn for their sins.

The Streltsy kneel down before the blocks.

116

КНЯЗЬ АНДРЕЙ ХОВАНСКИЙ
(Марфе)

А, ты здесь, злодейка! *(с гневом сжимая руку Марфы)* Здесь, змея! Где моя Эмма? Куда ее ты скрыла? Отдай мне Эмму, отдай мою голубку! Где, где она? Отдай ее! Отдай!

МАРФА

Эмму рейтары увезли далече. Господь поможет, скоро она жениха своего, что из Москвы ты изгнал, на родине обнимет.

КНЯЗЬ АНДРЕЙ ХОВАНСКИЙ

Жениха? Лжешь, лжешь, змея! Не поверю. Я соберу моих стрельцов, я созову народ московский, - тебя, изменницу, сказнят!

МАРФА

Сказнят?.. Видно, ты не чуял, княже,
что судьба твоя тебе скажет,
что велит она и что тебе укажет,
без корысти, безо лжи, без лести, княже,
и обмана...

КНЯЗЬ АНДРЕЙ ХОВАНСКИЙ

Эмму, Эмму отдай ты мне!

МАРФА

Гордый батя твой убит - казнен изменой,
и грешный труп его лежит непогребенный.
Только ветер вольный по-над ним гуляет,
только зверь досужий окрест бати ходит,
да только тебя вдоль по всей Москве ищут.

КНЯЗЬ АНДРЕЙ ХОВАНСКИЙ

Я не верю тебе, я проклинаю тебя! Ты силой духов тьмы и чарами ужасными твоими меня приворожила, сердце мое и жизнь мне разбила!.. Колдовкой обзову тебя, а стрельцы чернокнижницей добавят; на костре сгоришь ты всенародно.

МАРФА

Зови стрельцов!

КНЯЗЬ АНДРЕЙ ХОВАНСКИЙ
(надменно)

Позвать?

МАРФА

Зови!

Князь Андрей Хованский трубит в рог. Слышится колокольный звон.

КНЯЗЬ АНДРЕЙ ХОВАНСКИЙ

Что это?

МАРФА

Труби еще!

Хованский трубит снова. Под протяжные удары большого соборного колокола входят стрельцы с плахами и секирами, за ними следуют стрелецкие жены.

КНЯЗЬ АНДРЕЙ ХОВАНСКИЙ

Господи боже мой! Все погибло! Марфа, спаси меня!

МАРФА
(поспешно уводит Хованского)

Что ж не зовешь стрельцов? Ну ладно, княже, я тебя укрою в месте надежном. Идем со мной. Спокоен будь, смелей иди.

Стрельцы устанавливают плахи и кладут на них секиры острием наружу.

СТРЕЛЕЦКИЕ ЖЕНЫ

Не дай пощады, казни окаянных, богоотступников, злых ворогов!

Стрельцы опускаются перед плахами на колени.

STRELTSY

Father in Heaven, show us mercy.

(The Steltsy women stand behind the men.)

For our sins we repent, Father!

The Poteshny trumpets are heard offstage.

STRELTSY WOMEN

Show them no mercy! Make the bastards suffer, Great Noble Tsar!

The Poteshny trumpets are heard again offstage, but closer now.

STRELTSY

All powerful Father, forgive our sins and grant us thy pardon!

STRELTSY WOMEN

Punish them, stinking drunkards! Tsar almighty, show no mercy!

Trumpeters enter, followed by Streshnev, a young herald. The Preobrazhensky regiment enters. The Streltsy put their heads on the execution blocks.

STRESHNEV

(to the Streltsy)

Streltsy, your great and mighty rulers, Tsars Ivan and Peter, grant you pardon and reprieve. Return to your homes and pray to mighty God for the health and welfare of our rulers. *(to the trumpeters)* Now sound the trumpets! *(The Streltsy stand up in silence. The trumpeters enter.)* Tsar Peter will begin his royal progress to his coronation.

[26]   *The Preobrazhensky regiment moves off towards the Kremlin.*
The curtain falls.

The execution of the Streltsy as filmed by Vera Stroyeva, 1959

118

СТРЕЛЬЦЫ

Господи боже, пощади нас,

(Стрелецкие жены становятся за стрельцами.)
не взыщи по грехам нашим!

Вдали трубы "потешных".

СТРЕЛЕЦКИЕ ЖЕНЫ

Не дай пощады, казни окаянных, царь-батюшка наш!

Трубы "потешных" ближе.

СТРЕЛЬЦЫ

Отче всемогущий, помилуй души грешные наши! Смилуйся, смилуйся.

СТРЕЛЕЦКИЕ ЖЕНЫ

Казни их, окаянных, царь-батюшка, без пощады казни!

На площадь вступают трубачи и молодой Стрешнев в качестве герольда, за ними преображенцы роты "потешных". Стрельцы наклоняют головы над плахами.

СТРЕШНЕВ
(стрельцам)

Стрельцы! Цари и государи Иван и Петр вам милость шлют: идите в домы ваши и господа молите за их государское здоровье. *(Трубачам.)* Играйте, трубы! *(Входят трубачи. Стрельцы молча встают.)* Царь Петр пешью шествие в Московский Кремль чинить изволит.

Преображенцы идут к Кремлю.
Занавес.

ACT FIVE

A hermitage in a pine forest on a moonlit night. Dosifey enters slowly, deep in thought.

DOSIFEY
(quietly sitting down on a stone)

Here, in our holy refuge, I shall proclaim to the world the way of salvation. How I have suffered! How I have struggled with the whispers of doubt in my breast! Fear for my brethren and fear for the fate of sinful souls combined to oppress my heart, yet my spirit is steadfast and firm; may the will of our Father Almighty be fulfilled! Now the hour has come and my sorrow crowns thee, O my dear people, with the crown of glory. Long have we held in scorn the transient pleasures of life on earth, eager for joys of life hereafter. Beware my brothers! In fervent prayer we shall find the strength to behold the power of our Lord. God in Heaven, strengthen our faith if we falter, and we shall bring to Thee our souls not for judgement or condemnation, but for salvation in Thee. *(getting up)* Praise be to God! *(He turns towards the hermitage and prays:)* Brethren, will you heed the voice of revelation in the holy name of God who created Heaven and Earth?

OLD BELIEVERS
(offstage)

Most honoured father, trusted protector, gladly will we open our hearts to our God.

DOSIFEY

Amen. *(to the women)* Sisters will you fulfil your sacred promise in the holy name of God who created Heaven and Earth?

WOMEN OLD BELIEVERS
(offstage)

Courageous we stand, O Father, prepared to fulfil our pledge everlasting.

DOSIFEY

Amen. So clothe yourselves in robes of white, and light your candles in honour of God, and go forth to the place of holy martyrdom to suffer for the glory of God above.

The Old Believers leave the hermitage and go towards the wood.

MEN OLD BELIEVERS

Satan is risen, demon from the pit of hell.

WOMEN OLD BELIEVERS

Fearful is the Antichrist!

MEN OLD BELIEVERS

Prince of darkness, Lord of wickedness!

WOMEN OLD BELIEVERS

Death is near, prepare thy soul!

MEN OLD BELIEVERS
(in the wood, offstage)

Satan comes, defy his might!

The Old Believers come out of the wood and return to the hermitage. Marfa remains.

OLD BELIEVERS

We shall cleanse our souls in flames of glory.
In sacred fire, forever, we shall sing praise to Him.
Our Lord on high, eternal God above, Everlasting Father! Glory to Thee!
Extend Thy great power to make us strong.
Praise be thy name!

The bell tolls as they finally disappear.

MARFA

They've gone now, God above!
I can no longer bear my distress,
My heart profoundly suffers the pain of his cruel deceit.
Father, I love him. There's lies my sin, but hear me now,
I long to save him. Let me atone for what he has done.
I care nought if Thou should reject my soul O Lord!
Forgive me, O Lord, in Thy love for me, pity me!

ДЕЙСТВИЕ ПЯТОЕ

Сосновый бор. Скит. Лунная ночь. Досифей входит задумчивый, движения медленны.

ДОСИФЕЙ
(тихо опускается на камень)

Здесь, на этом месте святе, залог спасенья миру возвещу. Сколько скорби, сколько терзаний дух сомненья в меня вселял. Страх за братию, за участь грешных душ денно и нощно меня смущал. И не дрогнуло сердце мое: да свершится воля небесного отца! Время приспело, и скорбь моя вас, милых, венцом славы осенила. Жизни земной и преходящей утехи презрели вы, славы бессмертной, вечной ради. Мужайтесь, братья! В молитве теплой найдете силы предстать пред господа сил. Боже правый, утверди завет наш! Да не в суд иль осужденье, но в путь святого обновленья исполним его. *(приподнимается)* Отче благий! *(в молитвенном настроении обращается к скиту)* Братия! Внемлите гласу откровения во имя пресвятое творца и господа сил.

РАСКОЛЬНИКИ
(за сценой)

Владыко, отче, света хранитель, господу открыты вовек наши сердца.

ДОСИФЕЙ

Аминь! *(женщинам)* Сестры! Храните ли завет великий во имя пресвятое творца и господа сил?

ЖЕНЩИНЫ
(за сценой)

Не имамы страха, отче, завет наш пред господом свят и непреложен.

ДОСИФЕЙ

Аминь! Облекайтеся в ризы светлые, возжигайте свечи божие и грядите к стоянию, и да претерпим во славу господа.

Выходят из скита и направляются к бору.

МУЖЧИНЫ

Враг человеков, князь мира сего восста!

ЖЕНЩИНЫ

Страшны ковы антихриста!

МУЖЧИНЫ

Беспредельна злоба его!

ЖЕНЩИНЫ

Смерть идет, спасайтеся!

МУЖЧИНЫ
(в бору за сценой)

Близко враг, мужайтеся!

Раскольники выходят из бора и направляются в скит, одна Марфа остается на месте.

РАСКОЛЬНИКИ

Пламенем и огнем священным мы обелимся,
во славу вечную господа! Предвечного, бессмертного творца!
Слава тебе боже! Слава тебе!
Ты даждь силы грешным рабам твоим.
Отче благий!

Под звон колоколов раскольники скрываются в скиту.

МАРФА

Подвиглись.
Господи, не утаю скорби моей,
До днесь терзает душу мою измена его.
Боже, грех мой - сердце моя, услыши меня!
Жажду спасти я совесть его по клятве его,
и страха не поиму исключения.
Прости меня силою твоей любви, господи.

ANDREY KHOVANSKY
(offstage)

Where are you, my bird in flight?
Where are you, my one delight?
To your mother, have you flown?

(coming closer)

Are you dwelling all alone?
Where, oh where, has my lover gone?
Where, oh where, is my little one?
Are you dead or still alive?
Without you, how shall I survive?

(He enters, lost in thought.)

Emma!

MARFA
(to Andrey)

Dearest one! Canst thou not recall our first embrace of love? Since that time how many dreams have come to me: I dreamt a dream that thou were false and betrayed our love. Through this nightmare, how I wandered despairing!

ANDREY KHOVANSKY

Marfa!

MARFA

Be calm, my Prince! I shall always remain at thy side. Loving thee still, I shall burn with thee. Remember now, how we whispered words of love throughout the night, words of love that brought us joy and happiness. Now a cloud of darkness shrouds and obscures our love. Fingers of icy cold have frozen my promises. Now the hour of death has come, my love; I embrace thee here on earth one last time. Alleluia!

The trumpets of the Poteshny regiment are heard. Dosifey comes out of the hermitage, wearing a shroud.

DOSIFEY

They call to eternity! The time has come to win, through martyrdom, the crown of life everlasting!

The Old Believers appear from the hermitage, dressed in white and carrying candles. Some of them begin building a pyre.

MARFA

Canst thou not hear, afar beyond the forest, the approach of Tsar Peter's soldiers? We are betrayed, we are surrounded. There is no refuge, no hope of rescue. The hand of fate has bound us, chained us together. And has ordained the hour of our dying. And neither tears nor pleading, imploring, nagging, lamenting can change this decree, for fate is unrelenting.

ANDREY KHOVANSKY

Marfa, I beg of you, help me, I'm afraid!

MARFA

Let us depart, Prince, let us join our brethren. Soon the holy flames shall send our souls to Heaven. Canst thou not recall our first embrace of love? How we whispered words of love and happiness? The flames of martyrdom soon shall temper the vows that were made.

She leads Andrey to the pyre. The sound of trumpets comes closer.

OLD BELIEVERS
(from the pyre)

Father in Heaven, reveal Thy glory and might!

DOSIFEY

Brethren! The end is nigh! Reveal to us, Lord, Thy true divine celestial light! The carnal snares of the devil vanish in the radiant light of truth and love!

MARFA
(lighting the pyre with a candle.)

O God, our redeemer and our defender! Protect us!

The pyre burns higher. Trumpets sound closer.

DOSIFEY and OLD BELIEVERS

[27] Thine is salvation, everlasting. No power ever can harm us.

КНЯЗЬ АНДРЕЙ ХОВАНСКИЙ
(вдали)

Где ты, моя волюшка?
Где ты, моя негушка?
У отца ль, у батюшки?

(Ближе.)

У родимой у матушки?
Куда ж, куда я волюшку,
Куда свою негушку,
Да куда ж девать ее,
Да куда ж девать буду я?

(Выходит в задумчивости.)

Эмма!

МАРФА
(Андрею Хованскому)

Милый мой! Вспомни, помяни светлый миг любви, много чудных снов с тех пор видала я: снилось мне - будто бы измена любви твоей, чудились, бродили думы мрачные.

КНЯЗЬ АНДРЕЙ ХОВАНСКИЙ

Марфа!

МАРФА

Спокойся, княже. Я не оставлю тебя, вместе с тобою сгорю, любя. А слышь-послышь: жарко было, как ночью шептал ты мне про любовь свою, про счастье мое; тучей черною покрылась любовь моя, холодом, льдом сковало клятву мою. Смертный час твой пришел, милый мой, обойму тебя в остатний раз. Аллилуйя.

Слышно трубы "потешных". Из скита выходит Досифей в саване.

ДОСИФЕЙ

Труба предвечного! Приспело время в огне и пламени принять венец славы вечныя!

Раскольники выходят из скита в белых одеждах, в руках свечи; некоторые складывают костер.

МАРФА

Слышал ли ты, вдали, за этим бором, трубы вещали близость войск петровских? Мы выданы, нас окружили… Негде укрыться, нет нам спасенья, сама судьба сковала крепко нас с тобою и прорекла конец нам смертный; ни слезы, ни мольбы, ни укоры, ни стенанья ничто не спасет, судьба так велела.

КНЯЗЬ АНДРЕЙ ХОВАНСКИЙ

Марфа, молю тебя, тяжко, тяжко мне!

МАРФА

Идем же, княже, братья уж собралась, и огонь священный жертвы ждет своей. Вспомни, помяни светлый миг любви, как шептал ты мне про счастие мое. В огне и пламени закалится та клятва твоя!

Вводит Хованского на костер. Звуки труб ближе.

РАСКОЛЬНИКИ
(на костре)

Господи славы, гряди во славу твою!

ДОСИФЕЙ

Братия! Подвигнемся; во господе правды и любви да узрим свет! Да сгинут плотские козни ада лица светла правды и любви!

МАРФА
(зажигает свечою костер)

Господь мой, защитник и покровитель! Пасет той мя.

Звуки труб раздаются еще ближе. Костер все более и более разгорается.

ДОСИФЕЙ И РАСКОЛЬНИКИ

Господа правды исповемы ничтоже лишит нас!

MARFA

Think, oh think upon our wondrous love!

ANDREY KHOVANSKY

O Emma! Emma!

DOSIFEY and OLD BELIEVERS

Amen!

All perish in the flames. The trumpeters enter, followed by the Tsar's Poteshny regiment, and all recoil in horror at the sight of the fire.

*The immolation of the Old Believers in the 1989 Vienna Staatsoper production
(photo: Österreichischer Bundestheaterverband/Alex Zeininger)*

Вспомни, помяни светлый миг!

КНЯЗЬ АНДРЕЙ ХОВАНСКИЙ

О Эмма, Эмма!

ДОСИФЕЙ И РАСКОЛЬНИКИ

Аминь!

Раскольники погибают в пламени. К скиту подходят трубачи, а за ними "потешная" рота; они отступают в ужасе при виде костра.

Audio and Video Recordings

The Rimsky-Korsakov version

Before 1959 this was the standard version of the opera, made by Rimsky in 1883 from Musorgsky's papers. Ravel and Stravinsky made an alternative version for Diaghilev in 1913 which appears not to have survived in its entirety.

A 1974 recording with a cast from the Bolshoi, Moscow, under Boris Khaikin uses the Rimsky-Korsakov orchestration: Krivchenia (Khovansky), Piavko (Andrey), Maslennikov (Golitsyn), Ognivstev (Dosifey), Arkhipova (Marfa), Sorokina (Emma); LDC 278 1024. A 1979 video of the Bolshoi production is being released (Kultur No 1163).

Previous LP recordings not currently available are on Melodia (1946, Kirov/Khaikin; 1951, Bolshoi/Niebolsin), Decca (1954, Belgrade/Baranovic) and Balkanton (1971, Opera Sofia/Margaritov).

The Shostakovich version

Working from a critical edition of Musorgsky's vocal score by Pavel Lamm (1933), Shostakovich reorchestrated the whole opera (Opus 106). A colour film (Sovscope; distributed in the UK by ETV) was made in 1959 by Vera Stroyeva, using a scenario devised by the director with Anna Abramova and Shostakovich himself. The film score lasts only 135 minutes but it includes the scene with the Lutheran Pastor. Shaklovity's lament is transferred to a peasant in the crowd and it finishes with a reprise of the Act One chorus and prelude, devised by Shostakovich specifically for the film. The conductor was Yevgeny Svetlanov, using the orchestra and chorus of the Bolshoi. (This adaptation was first seen on stage at the Kirov in 1960.) The cast includes Krivchenia, Grigoriev, Petrov, Reisen, Leonova and Gromova; the Persian slave girls are led by Maya Plisetskaya.

Also on CD are two performances with the orchestra and chorus of the Sofia National Opera. There is a live recording of Raichev conducting the Sofia Opera with Elenkov, Gadjev, Bodourov, Ghiuselev, Mineva and Marimova (GEGA GD 113/5). The studio performance (Sony S3K45831; 1990) was conducted by Emil Tchakarov, with Ghiaurov, Gadjev, Kaludov, Ghiuselev, Miltcheva and Dimchewska in 1986. It is a performance of the complete Shostakovich version.

The Abbado version

Claudio Abbado's performance of *Khovanshchina* (DG 429 758 2GH3) was recorded in 1989. The cast, with the orchestra and chorus of the Vienna State Opera, includes Aage Haugland as Khovansky, Vladimir Atlantov as Andrey, Vladimir Popov as Golitsyn, Paata Burchuladze as Dosifey, Marjana Lipovsek as Marfa and Joanna Borowska as Emma. Abbado made his own version using the Shostakovich orchestration, omitting the Lutheran Pastor scene and making several other cuts, but concluding with the Stravinsky ending. A video (VVL 0700153) of the Vienna State Opera production, conducted by Abbado, has a slightly different cast led by Ghiaurov, Atlantov, Marusin, Burchuladze, Semtschuk and Borowska.

The Gergiev version

The 1992 production at the Kirov, Leningrad, was conducted by Valery Gergiev, and is available on CD (PHIL 432 1472 PH3), laser disc (070 433-1) and on video (070 433-3), for which the soundtrack is superior. The cast is Minjelkiev, Galusin, Steblianko, Okhotnikov, Borodina and Prokina. It is basically the Shostakovich version, with modifications to the ends of Acts Two and Five. This is the version performed by ENO in 1994.

Yvonne Minton (Marfa), Gwynne Howell (Dosifey) and Robin Leggate (Andrey)
in the immolation scene at Covent Garden, 1982 (photo: Clive Barda)

Bibliography

Richard Taruskin's *Musorgsky: Eight Essays and an Epilogue* (Princeton, 1993) has been frequently cited in this Guide as the most stimulating introduction to this composer, with a chapter devoted specifically to the opera (which is reproduced in the booklet accompanying the Deutsche Gramophon/Abbado recording). Taruskin's articles in the new Grove Dictionary of Opera (London, 1992) on Musorgsky and on the opera are excellent introductions to the subject. Accompanying his essay about the opera is a synopsis, noting when each scene was first mentioned in Musorgsky's correspondence, and the ways in which they have been cut or developed in the different orchestrations of Rimsky-Korsakov, Stravinsky and Shostakovich. Caryl Emmerson's essay about the opera in *Reading Opera* (ed. Groos and Parker, Princeton, 1988) is a provocative contribution about this opera in a study of nineteenth- and twentieth-century librettos. Footnotes to her introduction to this Guide contain other references. The double issue of *Avant-Scène* (nos 57/58, 1983) is for French readers, with many illustrations. Currently out of print is *The Musorgsky Reader*, eds and trs. Jay Leyda and Sergei Bertensson (New York, 1947), an invaluable source book.

For the historical background, Nikolai Riasonovsky's *The Image of Peter the Great in Russian History and Thought* (Oxford, 1992) is a dense and fascinating account of how differently he has been perceived by succeeding Russian generations, while *The Making of Russian Absolutism* by Paul Dukes (Longman, 1990) contains a useful chapter on this period. For a brief introduction, refer to Stephen J. Lee's Lancaster Pamphlet on *Peter the Great* (Routledge, 1993). Archpriest Avvakum's autobiography (*The Life written by Himself*), in an edition and translation by Kenneth N. Brostrom, is a Michigan Slavic Publication no. 4, Dept of Slavic Languages and Literatures, University of Michigan, Ann Arbor, 1979 (ISBN 0-930042-33-6).

Contributors

Caryl Emerson is Professor of Slavic Languages and Literatures at Princeton University, where she is also the Director of Graduate Studies.

Gerard McBurney is a composer, broadcaster and writer with a special interest in Russian music.

Rosamund Bartlett is an Assistant Professor of Slavic Languages and Literatures at the University of Michigan.

Carol Borah Palca is on the Faculty of the Peabody Conservatory of Music in Baltimore, Maryland, as Music Director of the opera department. She has translated several operas including *Hansel and Gretel*, Cesti's *Orontea*, *The Sorrows of Young Werther* by Von Böse and *Oedipus* by Wolfgang Rihm.